CLAIM
YOUR HERITAGE

POTENTIALS
GUIDES FOR PRODUCTIVE LIVING

Wayne E. Oates, General Editor

CLAIM YOUR HERITAGE

by

MYRON C. MADDEN

THE WESTMINSTER PRESS
Philadelphia

Scripture quotations from the Revised Standard Version of the Bible are copyrighted 1946, 1952, © 1971, 1973 by the Division of Christian Education of the National Council of the Churches of Christ in the U.S.A. and are used by permission.

Book design by Alice Derr

First edition

Published by The Westminster Press®
Philadelphia, Pennsylvania

PRINTED IN THE UNITED STATES OF AMERICA
2 4 6 8 9 7 5 3 1

Library of Congress Cataloging in Publication Data

Madden, Myron C.
  Claim your heritage.

  (Potentials)
  Bibliography: p.
  1. Christian life—Baptist authors. I. Title.
II. Series.
BV4501.2.M3228 1984   248.4   84-7315
ISBN 0-664-24531-5 (pbk.)

To
Ann, my partner in cares and celebrations,
and other significant women—
my mother, Anna
my daughter, Julia Ann
my friend Anne, along with
Jo, Flora, Pat, Marcia, and Beth . . .
and to four dear daughters-in-law,
JoAnna, Sabrina, Dorothy, and Nancy

Contents

Foreword

The eleven books in this series, Potentials: Guides for Productive Living, speak to your condition and mine in the life we have to live today. The books are designed to ferret out the potentials you have with which to rise above rampant social and psychological problems faced by large numbers of individuals and groups. The purpose of rising above the problems is portrayed as far more than merely your own survival, merely coping, and merely "succeeding" while others fail. These books with one voice encourage you to save your own life by living with commitment to Jesus Christ, and to be a creative servant of the common good as well as your own good.

In this sense, the books are handbooks of ministry with a new emphasis: coupling your own well-being with the well-being of your neighbor. You use the tools of comfort wherewith God comforts you to be a source of strength to those around you. A conscious effort has been made by each author to keep these two dimensions of the second great commandment of our Lord Jesus Christ in harmony with each other.

The two great commandments are summarized in Luke 10:25-28: "And behold, a lawyer stood up to put him to the test, saying, 'Teacher, what shall I do to inherit eternal life?'

He said to him, 'What is written in the law? How do you read?' And he answered, 'You shall love the Lord your God with all your heart, and with all your soul, and with all your strength, and with all your mind; and your neighbor as yourself.' And he said to him, 'You have answered right; do this, and you will live.' "

Underneath the two dimensions of neighbor and self there is also a persistent theme: The only way you can receive such harmony of thought and action is by the intentional re-centering of your life on the sovereignty of God and the rapid rejection of all idols that would enslave you. The theme, then, of this series of books is that these words of Jesus are the master guides both to the realization of your own potentials and to productive living in the nitty-gritty of your day's work.

The books in this series are unique, and each claims your attention separately in several ways.

First, these books address great social issues of our day, but they do so in terms of your own personal involvement in and responses to the problems. For example, the general problem of the public school system, the waste in American consumerism, the health hazards in a lack of rest and vocational burnout, the crippling effects of a defective mental outlook, and the incursion of Eastern mystical traditions into Western Christian activism are all larger-than-life issues. Yet each author translates the problem into the terms of day-to-day living and gives concrete guidelines as to what you can do about the problem.

Second, these books address the undercurrent of helplessness that overwhelming epidemic problems produce in you. The authors visualize you throwing up your hands and saying: "There is nothing *anyone* can do about it." Then they show you that this is not so, and that there are things *you* can do about it.

Third, the authors have all disciplined themselves to stay off their own soapboxes and to limit oratory about how awful the world is. They refuse to stop at gloomy diagnoses of incurable conditions. They go on to deal with your potentials for changing yourself and your world in very specific ways. They do not let you, the reader, off the hook with vague, global utterances and generalized sermons. They energize you with a sense of hope that is generated by basic information, clear decision-making, and new directions taken by you yourself.

Fourth, these books get their basic interpretations and recommendations from a careful plumbing of the depths of the power of faith in God through Jesus Christ. They are not books that leave you with the illusion that you can lift yourself and your world by pulling hard at your own bootstraps. They energize and inspire you through the hope and strength that God in Christ is making available to you through the wisdom of the Bible and the presence of the living Christ in your life. Not even this, though, is presented in a namby-pamby or trite way. You will be surprised with joy at the freshness of the applications of biblical truths which you have looked at so often that you no longer notice their meaning. You will do many "double takes" with reference to your Bible as you read these books. You will find that the Bread of Life is not too holy or too good for human nature's daily food.

In this book by Myron Madden, you find a profound and direct message encouraging you to push past your inheritance and heritage in your earthly family to your heritage in God's creation of you. You have here a compassionate analysis of the process toward claiming your heritage and affirming its strengths. You are not belabored with all the dark negativities of your existence. You are led to the refreshing oases of your potentials for creative living.

You will experience Madden's mystical and poetic flashes of insight, surprising you with joy, wisdom, and humor. Out of the crucible of his own suffering he has refined a gentle wisdom that you will want to read, mark, and inwardly digest. You will not just read this book once, you will reread it often. That is what I will do with my copy.

WAYNE E. OATES

Louisville, Kentucky

Preface

"Inheritance" includes gifts or bequests of property, genetic qualities, and the intangibles of tradition. The word "heritage" is roughly synonymous and includes all the above items, but it places more emphasis on the intangible factors, including language, culture, government, and social structures, and both the blessing and curse of certain relationships.

When I speak of claiming inheritance and heritage, I am assuming that there are liabilities in our personal past and in our culture that we would eliminate, if we had the choice. However, I am also assuming that both the gifts of inheritance (especially genetic ones) and the past influences of the culture are already a part of who we are, whether we affirm or deny them. Liabilities that we deny may become double liabilities; yet if they can be owned, they often become positive factors in the living of our lives. An example is the man who does not claim his male identity but rejects it out of his earlier childhood experience. He can live out his days rejecting his predetermined role, but he will not succeed in eliminating physically a role he rejects psychologically. Along this path he doubles his own burden by way of self-rejection. There are some things in our inheritance that are fixed, such as sex, race, nationality, and intelligence. We do well to ac-

cept the fixed and save our energies for the fluid and change-
able areas.

A woman can't do anything about whether she will be a
woman. The choice left to her is deciding what kind of
woman she will become. In claiming all that is hers out of
inheritance and heritage, what she likes as well as what she
dislikes, she is then in a better position to put her life together with others of the same pilgrimage. It is to be hoped
that it is a pilgrimage of denying herself the right to be anyone other than the self that was given in the beginning.

The spiritual task for each of us, then, is the task of claiming and owning the self we are and rejecting the temptation
to eliminate that part of our self or our history that we don't
like. There is not another person out there whom we fully
like, and there is not one of us who likes everything about
ourselves. But before I can change what I dislike, I must accept that what I dislike *is* there. I need to own it.

It is much easier to project my dislike of myself onto others who have the same weakness. I can see my weakness first
in others. Perhaps in saying "love your enemies," Jesus was
giving us the challenge of getting acquainted with ourselves
and recognizing that our dislike of others is a dislike of the
self.

When I own what I dislike in myself and in my heritage I
take the first big step toward healing a fragmented person.

Chapter 1

Your Self, Your Identity, and Your Inheritance

The intent of this book is to help you reach a fuller spiritual maturity, grow toward that maturity. It means claiming all that is in your heritage and history as a part of who you are. It also means finding ways to claim your potential in the unfolding process of life, allowing no essential break between your origin and your destiny. The integration of life calls for bringing it all together as your spiritual task. I will make a beginning definition of spiritual maturity as I understand it.

Moving Toward Spiritual Maturity

Spiritual maturity is recognizing that the roles we play on life's stage are temporary and transient, but it is also claiming and acting well the parts we choose or are assigned. Onstage the characters differ sharply; one may be king, another prince, still another merchant, clown, maid, prophet, or pauper. But when the act is over they all go backstage and mingle on the same level.

In the play the costume is everything, pointing out the differences between the actors. Perhaps in real life God allows us to display our costumes like children at their games. I doubt if he blesses such differences as male, female; white, black; rich, poor.

So by the grace of God we make spiritual growth as we learn to wear the costumes of our earthly differences loosely that we may lay them aside when the curtain falls.

Our inheritance as human beings means we have a great gift at the beginning of life and especially at the beginning of our awareness. It is the awareness of being a self that is the foundation of all else. Along with self-awareness goes awareness of others, and awareness of others starts a lifelong process of comparison and competition.

Venturing Out

We look at someone else who may have certain advantages in the realm of material goods, social prestige, or political power. These things often come by virtue of parental position and family fortune. Others are less fortunate in these matters. Two people never have an equal start in life; one always has more or less. It is not even the same between brothers and sisters in the same family. If there would be an equal beginning, it would seem to be in the case of twins. Yet consider the case of the twin brothers Jacob and Esau in the Old Testament (Gen. 25:28). In that case the special birthright and blessing as well as the material benefits went to Jacob. The course of their lives certainly was not parallel; there was an ever-widening gap between them. Even though Jacob was forced to leave, his growth began when he went out from the security and protection of home. He fled into the land of Haran to escape his brother, who had vowed to kill him.

We seldom grow spiritually unless we venture forth from our place of birth. Growth comes in the challenge of new experience. Joseph Campbell relates (pp. 245–246) the universal need of all persons to break from their primary center of origin, their family and their culture, and make "passage" over the narrow threshold from their place of beginning.

This act is best cloaked in terms of death and rebirth. He says all world heroes symbolically go out in search of truth, the Holy Grail, or the fire of the gods, or on some conquest. They receive a "call" but are tempted to stay in the place of comfort and security. The hero goes forth and finds a sign or a guide to the place of conquest. After the triumph, the hero returns to the place of origin, thus symbolizing a bringing together and integrating into one person the many and varied experiences of existence. (See Selected Bibliography for the full reference for this and other quoted sources.)

Expanding Our Identity

We are unable to integrate who we are until we expand our horizons. It is the call to "leave father and mother," or, as in the case of Abraham, to "go from . . . your kindred and your father's house to the land that I will show you" (Gen. 12:1). We are not usually satisfied with the identity we get from our parents. The spiritual call is always one of expanding our first identity to take on a larger one, and that usually challenges us to identify with persons of differing backgrounds and experiences.

Jesus could find kinship beyond his immediate family. When he was told that his mother and brothers had come to talk with him, he responded, "My mother and my brothers are those who hear the word of God and do it" (Luke 8:21). By this he meant that his family had greatly expanded. He did not limit his claim of kinship to those of his ethnic group but included Samaritans, the Syrophoenician woman, and the Roman centurion whose servant was sick. He was in touch with the truly human that is in everyone. He was mindful that the blessing of Abraham was for "all the families of the earth" (Gen. 12:3). In making himself at home with people of other traditions, Jesus did not lose his own identity as a faithful Jew, but from that position he entered into the joys as well as the sufferings of all others.

Spiritual growth does not call on us to sacrifice who we are that we might wear a mask in taking on the injustices or burdens of others. Rather, it calls on us to be ourselves in a full acceptance of others no matter what costume they may wear. Spiritual maturity is the alertness to know that all humans are the same at the core. We keep on wearing our surface differences without allowing them to rise to the level of essentials. This includes such things as language, color of skin, age, sex, and social or financial status.

Getting Stretched

Spiritual growth, then, depends on our hearing the call to go out from our place of origin to another place. In addition it calls on you and me to leave the people who are our people in order to identify with people who are different. The call does not require that we forget or deny who we are and whence we came. Rather, it asks us to include those who are different as a part of our enlarged sense of who we are. We simply expand our own being as we are able to form friendships with those most unlike us in race, tradition, culture, and religion. They are also a part of all that is human. "Do not neglect to show hospitality to strangers, for thereby some have entertained angels unawares" (Heb. 13:2). This implies that when we cut out the one who is different, we may be shutting out God himself, or at least his messenger. His messenger often speaks the truth before we are ready for it, and we turn our backs while the truth *for* us is usually the truth *about* us.

The movie *E.T.* is an example of our being given one most unlike us, an extraterrestrial being who is humanoid but greatly unlike us, especially in looks—he is positively nonhuman, aesthetically speaking. The deeper success of the movie seems to be that we are awakened to our capacity to identify even with the nonhuman. This makes more possible the task of feeling open and caring with every human, a task we struggle with much of our time. Hence we come away from the movie feeling good about ourselves, giving ourselves credit for stretching beyond our narrow limits. We have discovered a greater potential than we thought we had. Once we feel kinship with E.T., we have less difficulty claiming oneness with all that is human.

Going Beyond the Past

Starting Where We Are

We are not called on to forget the self or to sacrifice the self in order to relate to a greatly different self. We always come to the other person with a history, our own history, just as the other has a history, a different history. The task is not that of becoming as the other, but one of understanding the other in spite of all the differences. We come with the assumption that we are both human, with qualities that are the same. The person other than you is always the neighbor, and the neighbor is that which is the same in us all. Martin Buber, a Jew, preferred to translate Jesus' command from "Love your neighbor as yourself" to "Love your neighbor as one like yourself" (p. 51). This keeps open the fact that love of neighbor is possible as we are able to make common cause with the neighbor, as we are able to get beyond the surface differences to the essentially human.

Remaining your own self in the struggle to understand a different self is a way of expanding and actually getting beyond your limits. "Certainly in order to be able to go out to the other you must have the starting place, you must have been, you must be yourself" (Buber, p. 21). The sacrifice of one's being becomes unthinkable. Of course it may take many sacrifices in order to truly meet the neighbor, but there is no meaningful meeting if the self of either is diminished, withheld, denied, or compromised. If I am going to be enriched in meeting my neighbor, we must both come together with our defenses down.

Wrong Roads to Selfhood

As I asked a forty-seven-year-old woman who she was, the reply came, "I don't know who I am. I just try to be what everybody expects of me." My imagination went to work, wondering how she came to the place of claiming no authority for her own being and giving every other person the right to tell her how to shape her life. This sounded like an unproductive act of self-sacrifice. We can also lose the self by putting our profession or role ahead of our person, or our achievement ahead of being.

I knew a woman who at thirty-two years of age had been trying to live out the life of her older sister for many years. When she was thirteen, the sixteen-year-old sister had died; that sister had been the sparkle of the father's eye. This woman told herself that if she stopped being herself and took on the full likeness of the dead sister, she would get her father's blessing. Finally, she discovered that she had been pursuing an impossible course and had great difficulty, at the age of thirty-two, determining who she was and claiming her adolescent self as her starting place.

The Risk of Becoming

There are many temptations not to be who you are. There are many options for departing from your own self, but there is always the need to return and take up the task of claiming and being the self that was given in creation.

Getting beyond the self calls us to continue relating to our origin, to integrate new becoming with all that has been. In some sense it means venturing forth with the birthright into the unknown. It includes what was said of Abraham when he was called, that he "obeyed . . . and he went out, not knowing where he was to go" (Heb. 11:8). His venturing out into dreadful uncertainty was a death to his past, or perhaps it was an act of choosing the future over the past. Our willingness to let go of the past somehow becomes the springboard to the future. Perhaps it takes a "leap of faith" to fuse past and future into a self that is unbroken.

Affirming Your Self Before God

To Be or Not to Be

There are always two basic choices regarding the self. They are voiced by Shakespeare in *Hamlet:* "To be, or not to be: that is the question." That means I have a choice to be myself or not to be myself. I don't have a choice, as indicated earlier, of being my sister or of being the self that others expect. Those choices are only phantoms to be chased to the point of exhaustion, after which I come back to the place of departure. To be sure, there are other selves out there who have it made, who are successful, who are competent, who are blessed, who are prominent. The tempter says something like this: "Don't be Jesus of Nazareth, the carpenter's son, the unknown, unheralded son of a peasant woman, but try on the role of conquerer or miracle worker. You can be great and powerful if only you will sacrifice your history and your upbringing. If you deny that you are the son of Mary and Joseph, you can dwell with kings and priests. Take off your coveralls and don this purple robe." In the light of all this, I think Jesus would say a person must deny the option of being any self other than the one that is. The choice is to be or not to be. There is no real choice open for becoming a different self, no matter how tempting the offers.

No New Self

Even the greatest hope in a new birth is still not a promise of a new self. Our task as a spiritual person is to become more and more the self that was given to us at the beginning.

This all adds up to the fact that my personhood cannot be exchanged for a more attractive one, no matter how hard I may try to become different. That is simply not an option offered, even if the temptation is everpresent.

You may answer that people will not accept you if they know you as you are. That may be a feeling, but it is not a fact. The fact is that we cannot accept ourselves when we are not willing to be ourselves. When we don't accept the self, we could be giving a signal to others that leads to their rejection of us. The only self they can ultimately accept is the one that is real, never the one that is pretentious, artificial, or off center. God affirmed what he created in the beginning and gives us the freedom to affirm the self he gave to us. He does not give us the freedom to replace it, or the freedom to start all over.

I Am What I Am

As already indicated, we humans are reluctant to accept ourselves as we are. We also have difficulty accepting others as they are. This is more tellingly true within the close circle of family relationships. We often lay down perfectionist goals for mates and children. We seem to assume that if we accept our mates as they are, they will never change. Parents are reluctant to support a child with failing grades for fear that this rewards deviant behavior, even when the bad grades seem to be a cry for help.

There is a logic that seems to say, "I will love you after you show me you can do better." The mate or the child seems to answer, "After you show me you love me, I will try much harder to please you."

We all need to be accepted for what and who we are. We all need to be loved as we are. Our heritage has already spoken when we come to our first awareness of being a self. Some things are already fixed before we come to own them, things such as sex, race, siblings, language, religious influence, and economic conditions. Along with these go intelligence, talents, physical size, and stamina.

In making the choice to be who we are, we discover that we are limited by birth and environment on many counts. In choosing to become who we are, we do well to assess both the limitations and the possibilities. We become a more real self as we accept our limitations and as we claim the possibilities that are within our reach.

Chapter 2

Your Sense of Justice and Your Heritage

In Chapter 1, I affirmed the likeness, or sameness, of all human beings. A common bond of kinship ties us together in our human condition. But at the same time that I affirm our likeness, I feel constrained to affirm also that we are all different. None of us is the same as another, not even identical twins; each of us has an individuality that is never repeated. The paradox, then, is that we are all alike and we are all different. We are more alike than we know and more unique at the same time. The paradox might be stated in a more complicated formula: The more we fear to be different, the more we become the same as all the others; the more we accept being the same as all the others, the more unique we become.

Facing the Paradox of Self

Perhaps we take comfort in feeling our commonality with all the others. Yet we run into trouble when we compare ourselves unfavorably with another person or group. There arises a sense of injustice. Let me illustrate. There was a graduate student who was at the end of a long and disciplined study program and was about to take a very lucrative position in industry. He read of a gang of drug smugglers who had taken high risks to bring drugs from South America and sell them in the United States. Several of them were caught and imprisoned for four to five years. But as soon as they completed their sentences, each of them would be worth several million dollars. The student's sense of justice was outraged. It seemed to him that the drug smugglers were really ahead of him in the game of life, and yet none of them had gone beyond high school. On the other hand, he had put in ten years of college and postgraduate work. It was just not fair!

Alike and Unlike All the Others

There are many ways we feel injustice, especially when others surpass us in the struggle of life. We feel it when our neighbor gets a promotion and a new car or moves to a fancier neighborhood. We feel it when our peers bring in better grades, wear finer clothes, throw bigger parties, take longer trips, or win special recognition in the media. All these things stir our jealousy and envy, and not many of us have learned to manage such feelings acceptably.

There is an even more painful area of inequality: physical appearance. Shakespeare's Richard III is a classic example of an envious person turned villain because of his twisted frame. Tradition held that Richard III issued forth after two years in his mother's womb, with hair down to his shoulders and a full set of teeth. At any rate, Shakespeare has him say, after deploring his own ugliness:

> And therefore, since I cannot prove a lover
> To entertain these fair well-spoken days,
> I am determined to prove a villain.

In addition to the Richards, there are all those who carry some obvious or even hidden mark of difference. I have known people who felt cheated of their birthright for such things as short thumbs, a large nose, webbed toes, freckles, or a wart in the wrong place. Alfred Adler based much of his

psychology on what he called "organ inferiority." By this he
meant that a person would develop a rather general feeling
of inadequacy because of some unique feature of organ, skin,
or limb. It is as if the deficiency in one area spread to the
whole person. The greatness of Shakespeare's insight is that
he brings his characters to struggle with the injustice of being grossly different from other people. They are forced onto
the stage of life without proper preparation, like Richard,
"sent before my time into this breathing world, scarce half
made up." Some feel they have to act their parts before they
get their costumes and their makeup ready.

From these and other special conditions, many persons
feel that injustice is their lot. If they feel this strongly, they
tend to take justice into their own hands one way or another. They feel justified in doing injustice.

Alike and Unlike in the Family

Perhaps the first outrage over injustice comes in the family setting. We can be grateful that things have changed from
Old Testament days regarding the dividing of an inheritance. The rule then was for the eldest son to be given a
"double portion" of the family estate. Daughters were not included in the division unless there were no sons.

In the modern family, the inheritance is usually divided
equally among all children, male and female. Brothers and
sisters in a family may argue and fall out over the division of
property at the death of parents. But the property usually
represents something much deeper—namely, the feelings
that might have been given to one child and withheld from
another. I have a lawyer friend who maintains that the un-
loved child holds out for a larger share of the inheritance to
make up for what he or she missed in the area of affection
and nurture.

Neighbors are quite aware of the partialities we practice as
parents. They even try to help balance things out by showing more attention to the child or children they see us ne-

glect or forget. Grandparents, of course, also may get into the balancing act to try to guarantee family justice.

When all is said and done, we parents do show partiality, knowingly or unknowingly. If we are aware of being partial, we often try to conceal our feelings by making it a point to give more expensive things to the child who is less in the center of our care. That will throw the neighbors off quickly!

Norman O. Brown traces much human conflict back to the root issue of the child seeking sole possession of the parent—an attempt to own the parent bodily, as it were (p. 21). Of course the "ownership" shifts from an attempt to possess the parent to the substitution of substance: property, jewelry, land, clocks, or anything else that sustains the memory of the deceased. Family heirlooms stand at the top of the list as things that will divide children after the death of the parents.

I knew two brothers who were jointly willed the choice family heirloom, a grand piano that had been in the family for four generations. The father wanted to treat his two sons equally. He divided the property and the money evenly and without consequence. But the piano represented his blessing in a unique way. He left the piano—undivided, of course—to both sons. These two sons fought and argued for twenty years before they could work out a solution. According to Brown (p. 20), "The quarrel is over the paternal inheritance. But the paternal inheritance is the paternal body itself." For me, Brown is a bit too literal. I would say that the difficulty between the brothers over the piano was seated in the father's love, which they couldn't divide any more than they could divide the piano. The piano is a powerful symbol, representing how stubbornly we humans hold to our claim for blessing.

A true gift of the parental love and blessing is the gift that helps free up the person from the need to keep all accounts even and just. While Brown sees us struggling for justice, Erik Erikson slants the struggle more toward a search for blessing and affirmation. The one who gets the love doesn't require the love to be proved with material substance. One woman who knew herself to be highly blessed of her mother remarked, "I've always been the apple of her eye, and I would give all my inheritance if I could help my sister feel loved by my mother." Erikson puts the search for affirmation this way: "The child wants to be blessed by one important parent, not for what he does and accomplishes, but for what he *is,* and he often puts the parent to mortal tests" (p. 65). Erikson is quite aware of the changes taking place in recognizing that the child in modern culture seeks the mother's blessing as often as the father's. In my experience, the child—while taking for granted the parent who gave blessing—tends to seek the blessing of the parent who withheld it. Still another posture is one of seeking the blessing of the parent who carries more power or authority. If you want a simple test of which parent this is, see who the dog follows. Animals gravitate to the person who has more power, and they aren't easily fooled!

Of course we will never get complete justice, either within the family or in the social order. However, this gives us no excuse to turn our backs on injustice, no matter where it occurs. Let us hope that we identify with "even-handed" justice *(Macbeth),* the kind Jesus also recognized in God, who makes his sun rise on both the good and the evil and the rain to fall on both the just and the unjust (Matt. 5:45).

Justice and the Exceptions

Conditions That Make for Exceptions

Wherever people feel cheated or victimized by the strokes of "outrageous fortune," they tend to justify stepping in to put things right. This feeling of being cheated can be traced to a birth defect, an illness, or some condition that interrupts a more normal flow of life for them.

Richard III feels it is OK to do any injustice he chooses

because of the injustice he feels was done to him, "cheated of feature by dissembling nature." In assuming he has been cheated, he assumes he has a license to do what he pleases to reward himself for injuries suffered at the hand of an unjust order. If we press it to a theological frame, we may assume that God has mistreated us, and for that he owes it to us to put none of the moral and ethical demands upon us that he requires of the rest of the human family. The lesson here is that neither the conditions of our lives nor the paltry circumstances of existence give us an indulgence to do as we please. We are not excused from the rules, even when the extremes of circumstance prove to be most unfavorable to us.

Crises That Make for Exceptions

In addition to many conditions outside our control that make life seem unfair to us or to our group, there are crises that aggravate the feelings of injustice.

One type of crisis is that of natural disaster. This can be an earthquake in which all the savings and accumulations of generations suddenly go down in rubble. In addition to earthquakes, there are other natural calamities that deprive persons of normal existence. These include tornadoes, hurricanes, drought, floods, ravaging fires, and plagues of all sorts. We respond to these crises by declaring a disaster area, which allows the federal government to make low-interest disaster loans to the victims. This action comes from an assumption that persons who are victims of natural calamities need to be compensated by the government (that is, by those of us who were unharmed). This is another way of affirming that one purpose of government is "to establish justice."

Another type of disaster is that which results from human action. An example is the terrorist attack, where a few suffer for the many. Nuclear accident looms large as yet another possibility. War and the ravages of war have always stood as a threat to social stability and national productivity. The Arab oil embargo of the 1970s is an example of how helpless we all felt as the price of gasoline skyrocketed before our eyes. We might have felt justified in finding some sort of retaliation, but none was forthcoming. We felt we suffered from an injustice that we couldn't even address at any level. While we expressed anger at the Arabs, we noted the earnings reports of the major oil companies showed profits soaring above 100 percent. Did they have any part in all this dirty process? How was justice to be served?

It seems better if we can excuse ourselves from the regular requirements and expectations of society when we have injuries or losses from some sort of crisis. A crisis makes our excuse feel more excusable in the eyes of others. Yet we become incensed when others take advantage of a crisis in order to fatten their lives or their purses, such as looters after a tornado.

Rights and Obligations

Give Me My Part

In a critical analysis of our society, Alexander Solzhenitsyn says, "It is time, in the West, to defend not so much human rights as human obligations" (p. 21).

We not only have a right to *get* (in inheritance and heritage), but also a social and spiritual responsibility to *give*. As long as it is, for us, more blessed to get than to give, we may remain closed to our better opportunities.

A man asked Jesus for help in getting his brother to divide the family inheritance (Luke 12:13). That man wanted his rights. No doubt he was justified in seeking his inheritance. But you get the feeling that he put everything else aside in order to get what was his. Jesus would have no part in the quarrel. At first glance it might seem that Jesus was not concerned about a just settlement in the case. On further reflection, one wonders if there was anything that would give this man a sense of true values about life. His envy had no doubt eaten away at his spirit, and he could only pity himself for having been cheated out of a family heirloom. His only encounter with Jesus was used to ask Jesus to help him get justice, to settle the score with his brother. More than all else he wanted his share.

Special Gifts, Special Obligations

"To whom much is given . . . much will be required" (Luke 12:48). We may not be able to see God as one who gives the same to each person. There are millions, even billions, of people on the planet who are below the poverty level by any standard. There are many others who are able to bask in the sunshine of affluence. There is a very wide intelligence scale, with literally millions falling below the norm while great numbers excel in every manner of intellectual endeavor. Again, there are the gifted whose bodies support them in rugged physical competition, while others are born with little capacity to engage in sports or even physical labor. Any of these people on the lower end of the scale could complain that life is not fair. A mother says this when she has a hydrocephalic child or one with Down's syndrome.

We can cry foul play, injustice, or whatever in support of ourselves against our more fortunate sisters and brothers. No matter how we deplore the inequities around us, this does little to change our condition.

The issue is not how much or how little we get but how well we manage what is ours. In order to say this, Jesus told the parable of the talents (Matt. 25:14-30). It is a story of a man about to leave home for a while who called his three servants and entrusted money to each. He gave five talents to the first, two talents to the second, and one talent to the third. In due season the man returned for an accounting. The first servant had used his five talents to make an additional five, the second gained in like measure, while the third one, having so little by comparison, went and hid his talent in the ground to keep it safely for his master's return. Jesus said

that the master of the household rewarded the two indus-
trious servants. But he took the one talent from the con-
servative servant and gave it to the one who now had ten
talents. It sounds very harsh, coming from Jesus, for him to
picture a situation where people are judged and weighed on
the stewardship of what they have. They are not excused on
the basis of having too little. Perhaps Jesus was weary of
hearing how much better people could do if only they had
been born with more money, brains, privilege, culture, or
freedom. This is not saying he was unsympathetic to the poor
and underprivileged.

Stewardship is not simply a matter of managing money or
property. It is managing whatever comes our way that is normally felt as injustice. This includes tough conditions such as
poverty or the crisis of earthquake or hurricane. The experiences of life are our instructors, especially the painful ones.
Some people are able to use pain to bring their lives into
mellow relationship with their families and communities.
Others turn to bitterness, to drugs, to alcohol, or to some
form of diversion that prevents their own growth toward maturity or assimilation of the reality at hand.

The Stewardship of Heritage

Somehow the order of things in the natural world, as well
as in the world of business and politics, has never achieved
the status of equality for all. Many community experiments
have sought to create Utopias where all had the same amount
of material wealth, the same opportunities, the same privi-
leges. Communism is the most recent serious large experi-
ment seeking to bring an order of stable justice for all the
citizens. The problem is that those who have the power to
enforce equality do not put themselves under the restric-
tions they apply to others. This may not be so much a problem of communism as it is one of human nature. In all our
political systems we struggle to either legislate or dictate con-

trols of human nature to the point that all the people enter a peaceful, prosperous, and happy existence.

The issue comes up in every generation concerning a political order that will "establish justice" while promoting the common good. If we support the established government, we usually seek to improve justice. If we support a new order, it is to speed up the process of justice.

Various movements within the system in this country arose to give justice to the disadvantaged. An example is the labor union movement. Working people, finding life cheap and expendable in the face of big capital, organized to protect and advance human rights and human justice. Most such movements come into existence to secure justice for some smaller group. These groups sometimes do injustice to others to get what they consider justice for their members.

In the aftermath of the Communist practice of perpetrating violence to secure justice, it is becoming easier for some Christian groups to advocate the same type of action: a practice of injustice in the larger cause of justice. While this may bring immediate results, it sows seeds of resentment and hatred that will continue to bear fruit for many generations.

Obligations for Past Injustices

Some ethnic groups pass along their past stories of injustice and try to commit their children to programs of vengeance. This may become the consuming passion of children who seek to avenge past wrongs. An example of this is the almost complete annihilation of the Armenian community of eastern Turkey in 1918. The Turkish people feared this group and set about killing them during World War I. Of course there were a few thousand survivors of this attempt at ethnocide. To this day we hear of several Turkish embassies each year around the world that are bombed. Ambassadors and embassy staffs are killed. Invariably it is the descendants of those Armenians who claim credit for killing the Turks. It is the avowed purpose of many Armenians to punish for past injustice. One wonders how long this vengeance will go on.

Your heritage and my heritage no doubt cause us to look back on injustices done to our people, not the ones our people did to others. We tend to justify our own while we blame the "outsiders," whoever they are.

As a Christian I am called on to settle these ancient inherited hostilities and come to terms with the fact that the Turk, the Arab, the Cuban, and the Haitian are my neighbors in more ways than by living close to me. They all belong to the same and only human race. They all are a part of everything that is human. Until I am able to treat all other humans with respect and dignity, I am carrying around an inner block to my own growth toward maturity. My heritage does not serve me well until I can fully claim it as my own while allowing my neighbors to live in and through the heritage that is theirs.

Chapter 3

Owning Your Heritage

As I talked to a college Sunday school group about the birthright, one student with a look of fierce anger in his eyes and a quivering chin said, "I cannot forgive my father for his partial treatment of my younger brother and sister." He went on to say that he had been boiling inside over this since he was ten years old. I got the feeling that this young man was on the very edge of an anger that could explode into uncontrollable rage. He seemed poisoned to the core with feelings that burned and simmered. He felt he had a right to more justice than he had received.

When Things Are Uneven

We seldom come to adulthood without some feelings of injustice somewhere in our childhood or adolescence. A brother got more use of the car, the allowance was not even, the father went to watch little brother play baseball but never came to the school play when big sister had the lead role. We tend to keep an emotional record of the times we were neglected, forgotten, or ignored, but we more often forget the times when we were on the receiving end of special attention. We expected that; it was what we deserved. Our brothers and sisters were left with jealousy over those occasions.

Smoldering Resentments

John Steinbeck's novel *East of Eden* is a story of the bitter rivalry of brothers set off because of the partiality of the father. It covers three generations of struggle. The twin sons of Adam Trask reenact the ancient scenario of Cain and Abel. Everything about Aron makes Adam Trask happy, but he has no time nor thought for the twin brother, Cal. This gets Aron killed, because the unfavored son taunts the favored one, causing him to join the army, where he becomes a battlefield casualty.

This same theme appears often in the Bible. King Lear brings it into focus with his three daughters, giving favor to the flattering ones. Tennessee Williams demonstrates it in *Cat on a Hot Tin Roof,* a play that might have been named "a certain man had two sons" (Luke 15:11). In the Gospel we are reminded that neither family position nor personal achievement will stand after the curtain falls. "But many that are first will be last, and the last first" (Matt. 19:30).

When parents show marked partiality, siblings are set on a course of extreme rivalry. On the modern scene, we tend to discount the intensity of the strife that favoritism begets among children in a family. We read about it in the Bible and discount it as if we no longer behaved that way; we assume we are too civilized now for brothers and sisters to hate one another or for parents to play favorites.

When, on the modern scene, parents love more or give more to one child, that child becomes the focal point of hostility for the unfavored siblings just as in the days of Jacob and Joseph. We may need to listen more to the children who missed out on the birthright and the blessing. They usually smolder with resentment and have difficulty overcoming their jealousies and their repressed anger.

We have yet to learn the damage done to the human body when it becomes the disposal site of unprocessed anger and jealousy. I'm not talking about a periodic flare-up that must be contained so much as the never-ceasing flow of anger. This is the kind of love-hate attitude toward a father or mother that refuses to let go so that some sort of healing may take place.

The Unfavored Hold On

The sons and daughters who nurse a wound toward parents tend to cling more closely to the parents. This may mean that they remain closer in terms of space, not moving away from the hometown or the home state. If they separate geographically, they seldom do so psychologically. Their bonding to a mate is more tenuous because the unfinished business over birthright and blessing occupies first place. This also means that their bonding to parents is usually broken with greater difficulty. They may operate out of an assumption that they will one day accomplish whatever it takes to put things right. This again drains off energies that rightfully belong to a marriage in order to sustain it properly. Such persons seldom examine the false assumption that the birthright can be earned. They are usually like Cal in *East of Eden*, who thought, as a teenager, that a gift of fifteen thousand dollars to his father would heal the wound. But this only made things worse when the father refused the money. The blessing was not for sale!

The Favored Turn Loose

The other side of the issue is seen in sons and daughters who get the birthright and blessing. They tend to separate more easily, to leave their parents and go on with their lives. The blessed Abraham "went out, not knowing where he was to go." The call to him was to leave his father's house and the land of his kindred (Gen. 12:1). While he had a solid and secure inheritance in his father's house, he would surely forfeit his spiritual inheritance if he remained there. He had a faith that life was a venturing forth from a settled security to a wilderness of uncertainty. He needed to make sure that his

earthly inheritance did not stifle his development. At the age
of seventy-five, he did not let social security keep him from
risking all in the journey of faith. The "promise" before him
could only be sought wholeheartedly by giving up the security behind him. He had finished things at home in such a way
that he didn't need to look back or return. No doubt Abraham journeyed toward Canaan as a free and liberated spirit.
Having cut all the strings behind him, he was open to new
discovery as he pitched his tent toward the "City of God."

Coping with Partiality

Hurting from Hating

Returning to the young man in the Sunday school group
who said he could not forgive his father, I asked him if he
"could" not or "would" not forgive him. After a few seconds
of silent pondering, he said, "I guess it is that I will not forgive him." I asked him if he wasn't being hurt more by this
than anyone else. Then I asked him if he would be willing to
make the commitment before the group that he would forgive. Very reluctantly, he said he would try. I told him that
"try" was not enough. He then promised that he would do
so. This happened in a distant city, and I had no chance to
follow up, but I took his promise seriously and sent him to
do a difficult task.

Allowing Parents to Be Human

Let's speculate further on the case. I was asking this man
to turn loose of the thing that actually sustained him. But it
was costing him his freedom, his health, and certainly his
spiritual growth. He nourished his injustice as a spiritual tu-
mor that sapped his vitality and spontaneity as a human being.

My imagination also says that he held his father responsible for not being perfect. Perfection of parents is the assumption of all children in their early years. Perhaps this also

meant that the young man was determined to make his father perfect in spite of all the evidence that spoke otherwise. He must have constantly been deflated over the fact that he could not get his father back on the pedestal where, as a preschool child, he had put him. John Steinbeck says (p. 21) that this happens to all children, in one way or another, and that it is like the gods falling. "It is a tedious job to build them up again; they never quite shine. And the child's world is never quite whole again. It is an aching kind of growing."

I hope the student found within himself courage to see his father as a fallen human being rather than as a god: this makes forgiveness of his father as a human different and much easier. The next step in this process is one where the young man could, we hope, not exact perfection of himself. If he is like I am, he no doubt took a childhood vow to be a perfect father in order to make up for his own father's failures. If he could get release from his own vow, he would be in a better position to be a good father, not a perfect one.

If the young man can take off his childhood blinders, he will see that his father did the best he could, not the best he knew how. And so with our parents; they were once gods when their judgments were wise, their intentions always honorable, their convictions true.

Jesus' statement "Call no man your father" probably calls on us all to have the courage to see our parents as humans with both strengths and weaknesses. It also calls on us to have the courage to be peers with them, as humans not unlike us. They are often partial in their affection just as we are, or will be when we become parents. Of course Jesus affirmed that God is not partial; he allows his sun to rise on the good and the evil, his rain to fall on the just and the unjust (Matt. 5:45).

Forgiveness Includes Much

Forgiveness for partiality of parents is both a process and an act. The process is one of correcting our false assumptions, of realizing that our parents had no evil intentions (at least usually), that they are human beings who had to deal with the same problem with their parents. It goes back through endless generations. They had to cope with stress, with shortage of emotional and financial resources; they had inter- and intrapersonal conflicts; they had their own childhood vows to correct and their own inner-child-of-the-past to console or control. They were not so much *unwilling* always to do the fair and just thing, they were more often *unable* to do it.

Forgiveness of parents also includes, as stated above, forgiving them for being human and not gods. They probably never pretended to be perfect; this was something we expected. If we put such expectations on them, we do well in our mature days to take them off. We do ourselves injustice and even violence unless we remove them. We can't sustain a healthy spiritual and emotional growth if we use up our energies denying realities that are so obvious. All that effort costs us too much; the effort to clothe our parents in a glorious image is too much for humans to carry.

Anger at Your Brothers and Sisters

Easier to Show Anger to Siblings

Another angle resulting from parental partiality is seen when the anger is directed at siblings rather than at parents. Of course the anger is usually generated by parental acts, but many times the anger strikes out at the parents indirectly by being expressed as a brother-sister struggle. The sons of Jacob did not speak their feelings to their father when he drew the favored son, Joseph, into the inner circle of his affection. Their rage was spent on the little brother who outranked them with their father. He was a sort of eleventh-hour worker coming to the vineyard and getting more than those who came earlier. This always touches the human feelings of frustration and anger, especially when we are the senior workers. You might say that we secretly want to impose our own seniority systems on God. Again, it frustrates us that none of us has any seniority in the kingdom of God over any of the rest of us, contrary to the attitude of some seemingly mature Christians—especially if their institutions have seniority! But we all stand indicted. What we dislike most in the behavior and attitude of others, we will find in ourselves if we are both patient and honest.

The Power of Seniority

Back now to the family. The birthright in the Old Testament fixed a kind of seniority system, giving the eldest brother the place of authority next to the father. At least this practice guaranteed less family friction. It settled some things by authority of tradition. It made no allowance for talent, skill, training, or competition. Scripture does not reveal whether the seniority principle applied to younger siblings. I think, on the basis of experience, that it did. Perhaps we have seen it at work in modern families. The following story, told me by a young man, an accomplished lawyer, is an illustration.

He was the third of three brothers, all lawyers in the family firm. The father was a lawyer who founded the law firm and had died four years before. The eldest brother moved up to head of the firm, and each brother in turn moved up a step in salary and responsibility. This youngest brother said he had a better education than his brothers and, he felt, more talent and ability to go with it. Yet he could never hope to be head of the firm unless he outlived his brothers. He had recently been offered a position in another firm that would catapult him ahead of his two brothers and put him in competition with them. His struggle was in deciding whether he was being true to his father's memory if he took that job. He also knew he would incur the resentment of his brothers. Should he remain loyal to his family or be honest about his ambition for his wife and children? It was with great agony

of soul that he made his decision to break an essentially Old
Testament pattern, based on loyalty, and face the truth for
himself and his future. He took the new position.

I had no chance to study the feelings of the older brothers
as they were surpassed professionally by the youngest. I
hope they were able to forgive the act of family disloyalty.
But one can imagine that there were many troubled waters
to cross. The ancient customs are still with us; they have fil-
tered down through the centuries, and they give way stubbornly.

It is difficult to forgive what we feel to be an injustice, especially when it comes in the family among our brothers and
sisters. It feels unfair for younger brothers to succeed ahead
of older ones, for parents to give more to one than to another, for one to get special recognition above the others,
even for one to have children who surpass a sister's children
in school, athletics, or a profession.

In the story of the prodigal son, we see the father trying
to get the elder brother to forgive and forget. But that
brother "would not go in" to the party.

Resolving Anger and Jealousy

We all miss the party when we allow the family history to
dominate our adult lives. We tend to treat our peers as
brothers and sisters, our bosses as fathers and mothers. I say
we *tend* to do this. Our liberation from this does not come
about so much by our determination to change as in our ability to see and integrate the scars of the past. If we are blind
to the pains we tend to repeat them, and consequently we
change little.

Our health and peace of mind come more easily if we own
fully all that we have experienced of injustice, jealousy, or
anger. We can handle these emotions better if we see ancient patterns repeating in our lives as we deal with our
neighbors or our fellow workers.

We don't have to be so loyal to our own children that we

can't rejoice if our neighbor's child becomes the star quarter-back on the high school football squad. There is great maturity in being able to rejoice and even give parties for our friends in their hour of triumph. It is much easier to visit the widows and orphans and those in prison than it is to celebrate with those who succeed unexpectedly or unduly well.

Our love of neighbor is our ability to celebrate the neighbor's good fortune. Our love of self is difficult unless we balance it with love of neighbor, and this will tell us if we have cut loose from the ties of the past enough to truly own our history.

Chapter 4

Healing and Your History

Healing best takes place when life is rejoined, when past and present are put together. When my name fits all my history. When "I am what I am" can be said with an OK. This means that my redneck origins, the culturally deprived little village of my rearing, the poverty of my parents—all these things I tried to leave behind—are a big part of who I am. It was in such a depression setting that I first learned about life.

Against the background of my history I felt pressure to prove something. Perhaps that drive is yet with me—enough to push me into writing books. I hope that need has faded enough to get me on course with a childhood vow I once took to put the truth ahead of other considerations. This vow came at the age of eleven when I set out to read the New Testament, on my own and apart from the Sunday school interpretations.

Many Pieces, One Picture

Blessing What Has Been

Sigmund Freud has let us know the importance of early experience, especially the experiences we couldn't assimilate and had to repress. The steam from those repressed experiences gets in our eyes and fills our fantasies until we can be at peace with these hidden demons. The stuff of our nightmares and the substance behind our daydreams, these experiences need to be absorbed and used to stoke our engines and drive our machinery, but for many of us they constitute a counterforce, pulling against us with a dead weight. And we use energies we can't spare to drag them along with us every day. Consider the extra stress that puts on us!

It is our birthright, if we claim it, to be free from these hidden monsters that constantly feed on our limited resources—and often eat better than we do.

You ask, "But how do I get at the things in my past that I can't see?" I answer, "You don't begin with the early childhood stuff that is already repressed out of memory. You begin with whatever you know and feel to be unacceptable, and you make that known to someone, under God, whom you trust. You make that person your priest for the time, or at least your counselor."

The sense behind all this comes from the fact that the unacceptable bits and pieces in your history are stored in the same chamber as the repressed data of childhood. The sharing of what you do know and feel to be unacceptable is necessary so that the great experience of grace and forgiveness will come through another who knows its meaning and is able to communicate it.

When grace starts to work on the conscious monsters, it seldom stops until it either slays the unconscious ones or puts them to rest, perhaps into hibernation.

Wholeness and the Birthright

We confront a paradox in this issue of health and wholeness that comes out of division. To inherit the birthright in a human sense is to get your portion. Getting your portion implies that there was a whole that had to be divided. There are other brothers or sisters (or both), and each of them wants a share.

In the quest for our portion we may get division in the

ranks of the family or we may get fractured within ourselves, especially if we fail to get what we thought was our
lot. The division of an inheritance almost invariably leaves
some of us feeling cheated. Perhaps this is because part of
the things in any estate are measured in terms of sentiment
while others are given economic worth or value. No two children in a family put the same values in the same places with
the same weight.

A big step toward wholeness is a determination to put the
unity of things spiritual above feelings of envy over the division of property and possessions. I am not saying that we
ought to roll over and play possum when we feel injustice
has been done to us. We are obliged to insist on justice as
best we are able. However, working for justice did not appear to be the first priority with our Lord. As we have seen,
when a man who felt cheated of his inheritance asked Jesus
to intervene on his behalf, Jesus refused to decide between
the two brothers (Luke 12:13-21).

When the apostles fell into quarreling over their inheritance in the kingdom of God, Jesus let them know that the
decision in these matters was in the hands of God (Matt.
20:23). The very thought of inheritance, material or spiritual, brings human strife.

Healing and wholeness are in some sense our inheritance
in things spiritual. It is not sinful to divide the inheritance,
but illness and fragmentation come from human greed, a
greed that craves too strongly to have what our brothers and
sisters have. The distribution of lands or heirlooms is not the
problem; rather, it is the feelings of envy and jealousy that
arise where this is done.

A String for Many Beads

Acquiring Without Owning

In the parable of the rich farmer we see a fat, contented
man whose chief worry seemed to be bigger barns and bins

to store his increase. He pursued wealth without a purpose. He only wanted more. Alexander Solzhenitsyn accuses Americans of grasping for material goods in that same greedy way, without thought of what this does to the next generation. He says the heritage for our children is "limited freedom in the choice of pleasures" (p. 13). In other words, the younger generation suffers from a poverty of options as to how they will spend a weekend or vacation. Pleasurable opportunities increase, but there is too little time in which to operate. In other words, although affluence and choices increase, time remains limited.

Solzhenitsyn adds, "One psychological detail has been overlooked: the constant desire to have still more things and a still better life . . . imprints many Western faces with worry and even depression, though it is customary to carefully conceal such feelings" (p. 13).

All this acquisition brings on the question of the fat farmer when he faces the question of inheritance: "Whose shall those things be?" (Luke 12:20, KJV).

It is not a requirement that a man with great material wealth be happy, but it is expected that he will *act* happy. He is expected to uphold the illusion and, as Solzhenitsyn says, he will conceal his depression.

Many of us know people of means who worry more in making a proper division of their wealth than they did in accumulating it. But the wealth is not in itself the problem. The problem centers around the love of wealth to the neglect of investment of feeling and love in family relationships. When the wealth is all that is left, it represents the love spent to get it (whether it be much or little).

Blessing at the Core of Inheritance

When the question of inheritance enters the picture, children go for whatever represents the blessing that they missed as persons. Responsible love of a child, then, is the best guar-

antee that the child will be able to handle material value
without getting split apart over an inheritance.

I knew a man who was so much without love and blessing
from both parents that all the money in the world would fall
short of satisfying his craving. Since the love and the blessing were not available, he sought material wealth as a substitute. Yet in an unguarded moment he was able to say he
would give everything he had accumulated just to hear his
father speak one unsolicited word of love to him—a thing the
father had never done. He felt the father was unwilling to
speak it. I felt he was unable.

For another man it was this way: He was forty years old
and was running for high political office, having served in
lesser places of power and influence. But he lost the race for
high office and settled down to pay off his big debt (which
goes with such failures). He got into counseling in order to
better understand himself. He said he always, more than anything, wanted his father's affirmation and blessing, yet he
never got it. In looking back he realized he actually did not
respect his father, who had always been a very indecisive and
weak man. What he more deeply craved was the father he
never had, the kind who would take charge and stir up pride
in his children. In his own words he related how politics was
a substitute fulfillment. It became his way of getting approval from many people on a regular flowing pattern. Yet
he came to realize that this was never enough and, later, that
it could never be enough. He realized his own hunger for affection and meaning, or perhaps affection given with meaning. He needed a deep-level OK upon his being and person,
not upon his work and position.

The Threat of Nonmeaning

We humans hunger for the hidden meaning behind and
beyond the world of our experience. Mental illness might be
described in one way as having one or more big experiences
that we can't integrate with the other experiences of our

lives. When there is pain or loss, or anything that we can't merge into the flow of ordinary life, we may have to take time out in order to make such things fit. Existence does not come with labels attached to interpret all the parts and pieces. But the pieces of experience point to a pattern. The New Testament made the claim that the meaning was summed up in one word—love—and claimed that God is love. This is a thing none of us can see. We look at the jungle "red in tooth and claw" and at the social order gripped by fear over the split between East and West. On every hand we seem to experience two worlds, two powers, two loyalties; yet the New Testament insists there can be only one world, one God, one faith—that all words point toward the Word and that all pieces point toward a Whole.

If we have many fragments in our jigsaw-puzzle box of experience, it is most important that we accommodate them all. When we have some pieces that we can't fit into the pattern, we have to deal with this split that tears the world apart—in ourselves and among our brothers and sisters.

Healing as Outside Perspective

A bringing together of the self (and the world) begins in a venture from the primary center of our being, a move away from the self, as it were. We cannot understand the self until we leave our home or place of origin. To use a scriptural image, we must leave Egypt. There is nothing bad about Egypt in itself, but we have to leave it in order to know its meaning. It has a vital place for us all, but it can only represent the beginning, not the whole journey of existence. Egypt is the childhood of which many adults are ashamed, in the same way that children are ashamed of their younger siblings if the siblings remind them too much of their own earlier days.

You can know yourself better when you see yourself through the eyes of people from other groups, races, or religions. And you cannot see yourself through their eyes until you are able to get far enough away from yourself to identify with them. When you see life through a stranger's eyes, you are no longer a stranger to the other person. Seeing yourself from the outside means that you are more aware of who you are (see Chapter 1).

A Name and Making a Name

Straining Beyond Beginnings

The inborn drive to expand, explore, question, and understand is given to each of us. It pushes us out of the nest and into the mix of life. We begin with an identity that we feel is too much the one inherited from parents and home. We are seldom satisfied until we can add some material of our own to that house we call the self. We want to have a part in who we are. We actually need to have such a part. The common expression is *to make a name for yourself.* This includes making a claim to be more than we were at the beginning. It may call attention to qualities that others overlooked and add to our sense of worth as well as our worthiness of attention from others.

While it is important to add to the self in terms of achievement or development of our potential, it is important that we not stray too far from our origin. If our beginning was too humble or insignificant, we may want to deny who we were in order to escape rejection.

I knew a man who grew up as "Jimmy," a tag he always hated in spite of the fact he was James A., Jr. The first thirty years of his adult life were spent insisting to his friends and the local citizenry that he was James, not Jimmy. No one among his friends ever dared call him Jimmy, and from that group the word got out. The community learned quickly where he was most vulnerable, and what he most wanted from them or most desired from them. He despised his origin, his earlier identity as Jimmy.

We can repeat this story for a great number of other

people who despise such childhood names as Bobby, Billy, Joey, or Tommy.

The adult self cannot finally be accepted fully unless the childhood origin is included in one's identity. We are a part of every step of our journey, not just the adult part. In fact the scars, hungers, vows, hurts, and needs of childhood play themselves out in the adult with full force. The adult who does not know some of these earlier unfilled needs does not know the self that he or she is.

Healing and wholeness come in allowing the Jimmies to have their place if there is a half-grown child lingering in our history. The need to hide Jimmy under a more somber, serious, adult James tells the real story: the story that the Jimmy of the past was neglected in the haste to embrace the adult James and now must get his needs met by stealth or indirection. He must have his playtime, but it will always be done under the guise of something important.

The Nickname as Part of Us

The childhood name of which we are ashamed may be our nickname. The community is usually wise and kind (though not always) in giving a child a nickname that fits. But there is often enough laughter associated with the giving that such name can cause pain.

When I was a very small child, all my relatives and friends (except my parents) called me Tug. I had no problem with the name through high school. But college! I was terrified to think the college bunch would get hold of that piece of my childhood. They never did. A cousin went with me to college, and we roomed together. He had always called me by my nickname, never Myron, but I got him aside and swore him to secrecy about Tug. (It wasn't difficult to get his agreement, because he had a lot vested in his own nickname's being suppressed; it was one of those cruel names that bring more shame than blessing.)

There is some sadness that I lost my nickname. The power

of a person is contained in that person's name. The name represents the original affirmation of parents, a part of the birthright. A person's wholeness awaits the full acceptance of one's name. The name represents the merging of many forms and streams of experience. When the name can say it all, the name truly represents the person who carries it.

You perhaps have known a person here and there who would say "we" rather than "I" in speaking of the self. Of course this could have been picked up without reason from someone else. Yet I question whether the "we" person has all the selves together. A person now and then may strike you more as a "we" than as an "I," perhaps because of the person's scatteredness. There is one exception: The use of "we" by kings and potentates is proper because the role in royalty is a self most difficult to integrate with an ordinary human self.

The demoniac in the New Testament story spoke of being "Legion" in terms of the self. I had a mental patient who would say, when asked her name, "I am a thousand." I suppose the number here represented some attempt at holding the aggregate self in some show of integration, be it ever so loose.

A name loses some of its power when it ceases to include all the fragments and bits of the self. To put it another way, our name needs to represent our whole self. The wholeness of the self waits on a name that will gather all the pieces together, and such a name is a great gift to anyone.

Our Name and Our Birthright

Most of us are curious enough to inquire where we got our names. The juniors are rather obvious, as well as children named for mothers, grandparents, uncles, aunts, loving neighbors, and friends.

It is usually difficult to settle on a name for a newborn. You can't settle beforehand because you don't usually know whether to pick a male or a female name. If you pick one of each, that still leaves a decision after the birth of the child about whether your choice still satisfies and fits well.

In my experience of naming our children, I had a definite feeling that the name needed to become in itself a sign of a blessing. There was always much agonizing about naming a child properly, as if to name without proper care and thought would be to deprive that child of a blessing.

Most of us take the naming too seriously and give names that tend to be heavy, unique, or different. In being too original, we can give children names they resent or even reject. Sometimes the neighborhood goes to work and brings relief with a simple nickname. Some nicknames given like this may last a person for a lifetime, and they often suit better than one's own name.

We hope our name is just the one suited for us, yet often this is not the case. In any event, our name is part of our birthright, whether it suits or not. If it brings us pain, displeasure, or discomfort, we may want to find out whether we are rejecting not only our name but also much of our own history. That pretty much depends on whether we have made peace with our past, especially our childhood years. Those years might have been marked with unhappiness and unblessedness. They could hang over our lives like an ugly birthmark. It is up to us to claim those years if they are filled with fear, pain, or frustration. Since they are a part of who we are, they need to be owned and joined in an acceptable way to our own identity. If we cut ourselves off from our origin, we will be like a tree growing apart from its roots, a building torn from its foundation.

You can't rule out the element of chance and circumstance that can turn a good name sour. A cartoonist might pick your name for some funny or ridiculous character, a politician might have your name and carry it to dishonor, or a fictional person like the Godfather might do the same. Your name could become associated with a dread disease or with some person who creates a national banking scandal. No name is safe from one of these possibilities, but it is always good for any child to have an option: an acceptable middle name or maybe the blessing of a good nickname.

Jesus gave Simon a new name. He called him Peter (or Cephas), meaning "rock." The writer of Revelation must have had in mind the fact that, try as we will, we seldom give a fully adequate name to a child. So he pictures the final scene of our redemption where we are given a stone and on that stone a new name.

Chapter 5

Freedom from the Power of Your Inheritance

We are told that Esau scorned his inheritance or birthright, because a fragrant bowl of stew got in his way. He traded his future for a here-and-now moment of gratification. On the other hand, his twin, Jacob, was so in tune with future anxieties that he forfeited the present in order to allay fears over his tomorrows. In modern terms, Esau lived hand to mouth with little planning for his later years, while Jacob's insecurity made him spend more on insurance than on food.

Living Fully in the Now

Neither Jacob nor Esau is a good example of how to manage time and money. Each one lived on the extreme edge of his reality, one far to the right, the other far to the left. It was to the descendants of Jacob that Jesus said, "Do not be anxious" about tomorrow. I doubt if he would say the same thing to Esau's children!

Both brothers were controlled by their reaction to their inheritance; Esau scorned it and Jacob worshiped it. So it can be with you and me today. There are some who feel guilty about owning or inheriting at all. There are others who feel

they can never own enough. You need to deal with these extremes; either one can make you intoxicated.

The Influence of Past and Future

To scorn your inheritance is to separate yourself from your
history; to worship it is to give your history a significance it
cannot bear. As I have already emphasized, you cannot ig-
nore it and be yourself; neither is your past all that you are.
As a human being, you always stand between the forces of
the past and the forces of the future. This is not the case with
animals, since their present is not cast under the influence of
a projected future, one in which they take delight as well as
one from which they draw anxiety and fear. In contrast, your
human dreams tonight will be the meeting ground between
the unresolved elements of your past and the projections of
what you will do tomorrow and all your tomorrows. The living of your story, however you project it, is a part of your
"dream."

When the past holds too much terror, it keeps you in pre-
occupation. When the future looms with threat, you avoid
the present in order to cope with imaginary evil. You may
use up your resources either by fighting battles before the
enemy gets in sight or by doing battle again by bringing yourself back into encounters long finished. When either future
or past dominates, you tend to lose much of the present, the
now.

There is another way the present gets lost; it is in a
struggle with parents. It is not uncommon for the will of a
parent or parents to stir up the whole mix of life. Parents
may demand loyalty to their values. In a real sense they may
demand that you affirm their values on the one hand (all their
past) and that you do this in order to secure your future—
that is, your inheritance. You can pay a high price for that
sort of security. I have seen sons and daughters forfeit ca-
reers, change direction, give up the mate and even the children they loved, or sacrifice a lifelong dream, all because the

thing they really wanted would cost them their inheritance—or at least they were told that it would. They didn't want to rock the boat, risk the loss, or bring on some dreaded curse.

I will not say that parents have no right to do what they choose with their money and material possessions. However, I find it difficult to accept the threats and the manipulations that often occur in power plays to control the younger generation. I have known mothers to stop talking to their sons or daughters, to cut them out of family celebrations, holidays, or vacations. I have known fathers to grow sullen and withdrawn, even depressed and despairing, because they could not keep on influencing their children with offers of new automobiles or appliances. In one instance the parents grew morose and indignant when son, daughter-in-law, and five children decided they wanted their vacation apart from the grandparents. The grandparents took this not as an act of choice and freedom but as one of hate and rejection.

Risking an Inheritance: An Example

It is best not to be governed and controlled by someone's "will," in life or in death. It is not beyond your ability to let your parents know they can't control you by the promise of a better inheritance or by the threat of a leaner one. It is possible to pursue your own goals in life apart from funding that will cripple you. The following story will illustrate.

Roger G, a man of forty, along with his wife, Mabel, operated a business that was moderately successful but was always a struggle. Their own relationship was somewhat in friction because Mabel's father had advanced the initial money to launch the business. The father continued to hold considerable stock in the company. The couple decided to talk with me about their friction. My first question to Roger was to ask him who had his power. At first he contended he was well in control of his own situation and that nobody had his power. During the next session, however, Roger said, "I lied to you the other day when I told you I was in control of my own power." I asked him who had his power, then. He responded that his father-in-law had it, as a result of what Roger owed for the initial investment that put them in business.

To make a long story short, Roger, at the risk of endangering his marriage, decided that his father-in-law had controlled long enough. He bought the father-in-law out and took charge. This led not to greater friction between Roger and Mabel but to a resolution of much of their conflict. She appreciated her husband's show of strength in relating to her father as peer for the first time. In other words, they risked their relationship with the older generation and gained on every count, even though it seemed for a time that all might be lost.

Sometimes the risk of losing all needs to be taken, not in order for us to pull a smart one but in order to keep our integrity, to let others know that neither our present nor our future is for sale. There are always temptations on every side to relieve us of big decisions and scary risks. If the voices don't come from relatives and friends, they come from inside, warning us not to be foolish, not to venture, not to declare our own personhood. The voices are always there; they are not all bad. Some of them are our protection from constantly doing foolhardy things, like an Evel Knievel. There is a time and a place for everything, and it is the better part of wisdom for us to decide when and where to risk.

Our inheritance from our own family may or may not keep us from living the lives we really want to live. That comes as our decision and not that of our parents. It is possible for a person to do what pleases his or her parents most and still find pleasure in doing it. The issue is whether we forsake living our own lives in order to please others. This is a sacrifice we cannot make as Christians. We cannot sacrifice our being for a show of loyalty. Being comes first, being who you are.

That is the first call to anyone, as a Christian or spiritual person.

We are called on to make peace between who we are and what we own (or hope to own in an inheritance). We do not properly claim our inheritance if that inheritance comes to own us, to control our destiny, to determine our biggest decisions.

"Call no man your father" might have been said to free us from our past and our inheritance. But mostly I think Jesus meant for all of us, like Roger and Mabel, to have the courage to break through the generation gap and be peers with our parents in spite of the power of the inheritance.

The pathway to the here and now is liberation from bondage to past or future. As T. S. Eliot says in *Four Quartets,* we need to be released from the power of the old world ("Time past") in "the resolution of its partial horror." Then from the new world ("Time future") in the "completion of its partial ecstasy." Still, the present is lived between the forces of "the agony and the ecstasy." If we shut out the pain, we also close the door to joy. Living in the now includes having unlocked both the front door and the back door to our emotional house. It is getting to that place where we don't have to prove so much, either to ourselves or to our parents. This frees us from bondage to our heritage as well as to our inheritance.

Being Concerned with Call

Losing Much and Gaining More

As Christians we are not orphaned because we are called on to be peers with our father or mother—that is, to lose them in the sense of depending on them as a child does. Instead of becoming an orphan, we get a new family, with God as Father. We get a new center of things, a new reality. When we take the step of responsible adulthood, we are prepared to live as a peer with all adults, even the authorities of our society.

In dealing with inheritance, we are close to the market place of material value. This is not bad. But in dealing with our spiritual inheritance, we move to another plane or sphere. The law of the material world is at work; achievement, struggle, competition prevail. That law no longer applies in the world of spirit. Michael Novak words it beautifully (p. 59): "But effort is not everything. Life is also grace, gift, serendipity. . . . So many of the best, deepest, and most important turns in our lives were not exactly of our choosing, certainly did not spring from careful analysis, but came as gifts: the flight of the dove." The title of Novak's book, *Ascent of the Mountain, Flight of the Dove,* is a subtle suggestion that life is both the struggle of climbing mountains and the gift of the Spirit (dove), which is grace.

Spiritual Gifts

The first gift of the Spirit is perhaps the help for you and me to know that God wants to "give us all things" and that God is more desirous of giving than we are capable of receiving. The second gift of the Spirit seems to be the awareness that we already have more than we can own or appreciate. This includes not only our possessions but also our advantages in being exposed to an incredibly varied and beautiful creation. In our desire to own more of the creation, to hold title to more acres, trees, gardens, we might forget that ownership of such things is not so much the things registered in our name as those things we truly enjoy and celebrate. How can we hold title to the cardinals and the squirrels that come and go, or the butterflies in their haphazard flight across the lawn? Are they not a floating bouquet that no florist can match? It never occurs to a little child to possess first, but rather to take joy in the things of the creation. Perhaps Paul talks from the childlike mood when he speaks of "having nothing, and yet possessing everything" (II Cor. 6:10).

Another gift of the Spirit is the gift of loving the creation so that our children catch the spirit of love about all that God has given to all of us from the beginning—namely, a creation to take delight in as he did and does.

But the gifts don't end there. Human beings are even a greater marvel and mystery than all the wonders of nature. Shakespeare puts it well in the utterance of Hamlet:

> What a piece of work is a man! How noble in reason! How infinite in faculty! In form and moving how express and admirable! In action how like an angel! In apprehension how like a god! The Beauty of the world! The paragon of animals!

I'm not being prejudiced to affirm again a significant theme of the Old Testament that "the Lord's portion is his people" (Deut. 32:9). "Portion" (the same word as "share") is related to one's part of an inheritance. Human beings are at the heart of spiritual value, and we are given belief and hope that we are only on the verge of understanding how we fit into the large scheme. Shakespeare was not overstating the glory that belongs to human beings.

Being Where You Belong

Your calling as a Christian then centers around being yourself before God and the community set in the context of a marvelous creation. It also centers on your being who you are and not being tempted to become what it is not your gift to become. Many years ago, David Grayson, speaking as a farmer, put it well (p. 66):

> Joy of life seems to me to arise from a sense of being where one belongs, as I feel right here; of being foursquare with the life we have chosen. All the discontented people I know are trying sedu-

lously to be something they are not, to do something they cannot do. In the advertisements of the
county paper I find men angling for money by
promising to make women beautiful and men
learned or rich—overnight—by inspiring good
farmers and carpenters to be poor doctors and
lawyers . . . we try to grow poetry where plumb-
ers would thrive grandly!—not knowing that
plumbing is as important and honourable and necessary to this earth as poetry.

Grayson says the happiness and fulfillment of life depend
on our being "right with God or right with life," with the
feeling that my life is "absolutely necessary to the conduct
of this universe." He goes on to give his own testimony (pp.
66, 67):

I understand it perfectly; I, too, followed long after false gods. I thought I must rush forth to see
the world, I must forthwith become great, rich,
famous, and I hurried hither and thither, seeking
I knew not what. Consuming my days with the infinite distractions of travel, I missed, as one who
attempts two occupations at once, the sure sat-
isfaction of either. Beholding the exteriors of cit-
ies and of men, I was deceived with shadows; my
life took no hold upon that which is deep and
true. . . . But as I grow older, I remain here on my
farm, and wait quietly for the world to pass this
way. My oak and I, we wait, and we are satisfied.

Being in your place before God is not the gift of another
to dictate to you; neither can you be given that gift by ever
so clever a psychological test, nor by the wisest counselor on
record. That place becomes yours by your choosing and by
the gift of grace combined. You may not know at a given

time which of these figures first in helping you to "belong," as David Grayson puts it.

In dealing with heritage and inheritance I am not suggesting a way of asceticism, though I'm in no sense scorning that either. If we feel compelled to be divested of material things, that in itself could be a sign that we have not learned to walk through the world of matter without getting intoxicated. Like Pierre Teilhard de Chardin, I sing praises to matter and am glad to celebrate the infinite variety of ways it impinges upon us human beings. At the conclusion of his "Hymn to Matter," Teilhard de Chardin prays (p. 70):

> Raise me up then, matter, to those heights, through struggles and separation and death; raise me up until, at long last, it becomes possible for me in perfect chastity to embrace the universe.

Owning your inheritance is a part of the mastery of matter that it is your obligation as a child of God to bring under control. Either you will control it or you will be controlled by it. Your inheritance, so charged with both financial value and emotional value, can become the quickest road to temptation. Your soul may be most easily bought with a family heirloom.

Matter and material value are not all that you and I deal with in family. Sometimes there is no money, only a heritage as our inheritance. This can be a great boost; sometimes it can be a liability or a curse that we may need to master.

Living Beyond the Curse Character of the Past

A Curse in My Story

In my own history and heritage, not all was aglow with beauty and blessing. Over our tribe there ruled a patriarch, my grandfather. Now, my two brothers would stand me down that Pa, as we called him, was about the greatest guy who ever lived. He blessed both my brothers generously, but he passed me by, although I was my mother's favorite. My oldest brother should have been my mother's child of blessing by all normal rules (see my *The Power to Bless*). However, since my mother gave birth to her first-born son in the house of my father's parents, Pa blessed my oldest brother. This situation left me more in a bond with my mother. My parents moved their own home near my grandparents just after their first son was born. My grandparents kept their claim on him and continued the special bonding to that brother all their lives.

All this put me in a bonding with my mother but left me the target of Pa's wit and fun-poking. Now, some sixty years later, I can still hear Pa's words, spoken to my mother when he wanted to put her down. Referring to me, he said, "Why, that boy will never amount to a hill of beans." I never knew where he got the phrase, but a hill of beans of course was the description for two or three bean seeds planted in the same spot. For the very longest time, as I thought of going to college, Pa's words would ring in my ears and I would be filled with the curse of self-doubt. Was there any need to try? The old patriarch, the community authority, the family authority and prophet had spoken!

Getting Past the Curse

There are so many ways the curse gets released through the family. Perhaps you cannot relate to my story, but what about your own? I would like to cite some examples of other ways the curse got relayed and had to be overcome. Incidentally, I was able to get beyond the patriarchal prophecy when I was able to claim my own authority as being no less important than that of my grandfather. Freedom from his curse came by my declaration of freedom from it.

You might have been caught in the strife between your parents, finding yourself a kind of peacemaker, having to sacrifice your own life, needs, wishes, and opportunities just to

keep your parents together. You might have become their
glue or their scapegoat. There is little blessing in such role,
yet many children get caught there. If that was your heritage, you don't have to stay at the point of such bondage.
Again, the way out can come only by your decision and determination to rise above it.

I have seen the family curse come to children of divorce
as they got caught in a tug-of-war between father and father's
family struggling against mother and mother's family. Again,
the curse is removed when we accept that our parents are not
so much motivated by an unwillingness to bless and affirm as
by an inability to do so. When this reality gets through, we
can more nearly accept our parents as human beings like ourselves, not as the giants of the forest we imagined in our
childhood.

Maybe the curse on your family was the curse of politics.
That curse manifests itself in a need to look good not so
much for the sake of goodness but for the need to get votes
by not ruffling the sensibilities of the little old ladies in the
community. A friend raised in a political household told me,
"The political family will always be in church; they will sit together, down front, getting there early and leaving late." If
this was your heritage, you no doubt took a vow either to go
to church for the right reasons or not to go at all. The political family needs to look religious, committed, harmoni-
ous, happy, and contented. It is not necessary that any of the
above be true, just that it all seem so. Children in such a family grow weary of the facade, until it becomes a cross to bear.

Your curse could have been something more subtle, such
as a case of depression in one of your parents—your father,
for example. The depression might not have been so mani-
fest that he went around in a morose state all the time. It
might have been a less respectable depression, one that
manifested itself as laziness or sluggishness, so that he
couldn't hold a job long or make the money necessary to
keep the family going. Your mother perhaps had to pitch in

and get a job while she did all the housework too. The curse could be a vow you still carry many years later, one you made as a child, to help your father, to liberate him, make him happy, give him money. Perhaps he died before you carried out your vow, and now you can't forgive yourself for not having done more while he was alive. Only you can release yourself from vows you made. They remain a curse until you admit you can be OK even if you haven't done everything in life you said you would do.

Liberation from the many scars, pain, or terrors of your history comes in your ability to let it all work for you rather than against you. All this is a part of your story, and it is up to you to claim and use it. Under God's grace all curses can turn slowly to blessing—as the water can be turned to wine.

Other Factors of Inheritance

Beyond the Family

The illustrations from the family point beyond the family to our social inheritance and the stamp of regionality that is always a part of us. In grammar school, we got a perspective of the world beyond our mothers. In high school, we learned to criticize our sisters and brothers. In college or travel, we moved outside our community enough to evaluate it without loyal prejudice. In moving to distant places, we can look back on our home community or our region with some amusement. This is the meaning of Thomas Wolfe's *You Can't Go Home Again.* It becomes impossible for us to see the place of our origin as we originally saw it. Once we see it from the outside, we can't get all the way back under the cover of the past.

Our experiences and exposures to different cultures, languages, cuisine, dress, music, and so on all become at least a part of who we are. Such exposure always erodes our regional caste and color as we take on some of the images of those people who are different from us and from our earlier friends and family.

Owning and Claiming It All

If we turn our backs on our history and seek a new identity in a new place, we only show that we are enslaved to our past by our desire to be rid of it. This shows up when a person quickly adopts the dialect of any region where he or she might live, even temporarily. This usually says that the knowledge of the self, as well as the acceptance of the self, is still uncertain. In such behavior, a person is seeking to be known and accepted more easily, but this usually accomplishes the opposite of what was intended. When people talk the same language naturally, this brings an easier acceptance, but where a regional dialect is adopted, the people of that region control the time it takes for an outsider to be accepted. They will resent anyone's being able to enter their scene too speedily, even in speech patterns.

In taking on a new culture or a new life-style, the more healthy and wholesome move is that of integrating the new with the old, claiming and using the best of both, without shame of either. We express who we are through all that we are, and shame from others about change may be a sign that it still costs us too much to please either the authorities or our peers, let alone both.

Chapter 6

Freedom from the Pretense

No one can give you freedom. I once told a middle-aged woman with a marriage in conflict that I sensed her husband didn't have his freedom. She replied quickly, "Oh, yes, he does, I give him his freedom." If you are free by someone's gift or permission, freedom does not belong to you; it is controlled by another person or power.

Freedom Is a Declaration

Claiming Our Freedom

Freedom is not a thing you win in a war or a struggle, it comes by your declaration. It is too personal to be a gift of the state or any other power. It is good to live in a country that guarantees personal liberties and freedoms. However, persons who wait on the state to deliver these things will find that they have to be owned, claimed, possessed, exercised. Freedom is a way of living life, not of inheriting rights, as important as that is.

In order to be a free person, then, I must claim the freedom that belongs to me alone and to no one else. Certain freedoms are lost under a repressive state, yet there are some freedoms that no power can take away, such as freedom of thought. We may lose the freedom to publicly express our thoughts. In a repressive state this may force us to greater creativity. For example, there is John Bunyan with *Pilgrim's Progress,* written in prison. Also we see John, imprisoned on Patmos, writing in code in the book of Revelation. Not having freedom of speech, he exercised freedom of the imagination. In this way his message still got through.

Again, the state may shut down all churches and public gatherings in order to curtail free expressions of worship. This only changes the outward form of worship. No state can keep small clusters of people from gathering and celebrating in private.

When freedoms are not exercised, they are meaningless for us, even nonexistent. When we fail to practice being free, we are in danger of losing freedom.

Abuse of Freedom

The abuse of freedom can only occur where there is freedom. Frankly, the media church gives me cause for anxiety over the possible abuse of a time-honored freedom. I listened to an hour-long worship program on television one morning. In that hour, more than thirty minutes were spent on selling the program's value to the public and, of course, selling its books, tracts, and Bibles. The sermon that day extolled all the virtues of tithing. It no longer advocated tithing to your local church, as it once did, but solicited the tithe from the hearers directly. The program was showing signs of desperation, like a dying man who must use all his resources just to breathe. That experience left me with a feeling that this particular telecast was trying to be the church itself, rather than be a supplement to the fellowship of people bonded together in meaningful relationship.

Blood-bought freedoms, such as freedom of religion and freedom of the press, are constantly under attack. We do well, in exercising these freedoms, to make sure that we handle them as costly treasures and not as occasions to advance any private scheme, venture, or project. This applies not only to the media church but to the church at large. One responsibility of the press is to deal in truth, not propaganda. While it has freedom to print untruth, a free press must earn its rights over and over in an honest attempt to tell the truth, even when the truth becomes costly—for a time.

The Practice of Religious Freedom

The Practice of Freedom

I practice religious freedom when I claim my full right to be different from every other human being before God. It also includes my ability to identify with each and every person who pursues the path of individuality and difference. My identification with those who are different puts me in a sort of paradox as I seek the rights of individuals and the good of the larger community at the same time. Indeed, I may be driven to unreasonable decisions in the effort to preserve integrity of conscience.

Christianity, as Søren Kierkegaard noted in *Fear and Trembling,* does not put survival of the community as the highest value. Christianity cherishes survival, but not at the cost of conscience. There comes a time when a person goes against all reason to follow intense belief, such as Abraham in the sacrifice of his son Isaac. Kierkegaard insists that there are occasions when the individual may do seemingly insane things because of the inner voice of faith.

In the process of putting one's conviction above the law, one does not suspend the law. Even "Christ after the flesh" was judged by the law of the state and sentenced because he was thought to be dangerous to the orderly process of life in the community. When any of us puts conviction of conscience above the law (or custom become law), he or she will be liable to prosecution by the law—as were Jesus and Socrates. Jesus did not expect to escape legal judgment because he saw himself following a higher command.

In the late sixties we had an example of protest over the war in Vietnam. People were willing to protest what they believed to be an immoral practice in the name of national security. Many brave and spiritually-minded citizens suffered for what they believed and said. Suffering occurs whenever a person objects to the popular actions of the state, especially if the objection is on religious grounds. It usually threatens the powers of any state to be reminded of a moral law that stands above and judges its actions.

Freedom and Integrity

We have been speaking of the integrity that holds principle ahead of survival. This is the conviction with which Martin Luther said, "I can do no other, so help me God." In his stand of faith, Luther took the risk of winning the loyalty of many supporters. If he had failed, his life could have been at stake. John Bunyan remained in Bedford jail for twelve long years because he would not give the authorities assurance that he would not preach if released. Before his release, he was elected pastor of the congregation in Bedford. He went back and forth between prison and pulpit while his family suffered great privation. He refused to put the needs of his impoverished family above his moral and spiritual convictions.

Personal integrity is the act of a human being refusing to compromise his or her convictions in order to survive or gain power or position. The Lord asked, "Lead us not into temptation." Perhaps this meant, "Save us from losing our integrity by selling our self short or for setting a price on our personal power." Wherever there is power there seems to come a temptation to use that power first for personal gain, honor, or glory. Very seldom is the temptation one to *do* evil. The tempter wants control of the power and gets it by blessing it to be used for good purposes. It is the good we can do that often blinds us to the control of evil. Evil obtains power by permitting good to be done for the wrong reasons. The tempter seems perfectly willing to purchase human integrity with a guarantee of keeping a confidence. No one ever need know that a private transaction took place and that a soul was purchased, rather than a body.

It is no longer legal for us to buy or sell human bodies. But it has never been illegal for us to sell souls. The merchandising of souls is quite a business. The tempter seems to love control of those whose image is one of doing great good on earth. His greatest offer was in the wilderness, where Jesus gave us a model and example of how to keep our integrity. Jesus must have been thinking of this ordeal when he asked later what a man would give in exchange for his soul.

Truth and Freedom

The Truth Makes Us Free

We often hear "The truth will make you free." I believe that, but before it makes us free it makes us angry. This is the reality about how "the truth hurts." Again, Jesus said, "Love your enemies." This means get acquainted with the alien part of yourself, that part you despise in other people but neglect to see within yourself.

The truth is that my enemy is the person I reject who is much like me, yet is too threatening for me to recognize. My task is unfinished until I am able to identify with the person most unlike me, because this one, too, is very much like me. Finally, this is my neighbor whom I am commanded to love as myself. I cannot fully love myself until I love my neighbor (see Chapter 1).

Jesus says he is the prisoner, the orphan, the destitute. That means he identifies most easily with the ones in need. I find it easiest to identify with the ones in plenty. My bondage comes in my search for approval of the elite, the powerful, the prominent, or the rich. It seems that they can really bless me, whereas it seems that the poor of the earth have no power or ability to give me anything that would count.

But here is the rule: Jesus did not send us into relationship to *get* first but to *give,* if we would find our blessedness.

It is all summarized in how he told us to give parties. He said we should not invite our rich friends and neighbors, those who can return the favor, but rather we should invite those who cannot afford a party (Luke 14:12). To put it all in more realistic language, we are to look for those whom we can bless and affirm rather than exhaust ourselves trying to get the affirmation and blessing of the powerful and important people of the community. They are usually obsessed with their own power and status to such a degree that they really are not able to bend to ordinary needs and hungers. They are, in fact, out seeking blessing and approval because their hunger for approval is often greater than the average. Sometimes the higher their position, the hungrier they are—even if they pose as full and contented, ready to bless and affirm all the people they encounter.

Another truth for me is the fact that I need to go on a diet about my need to be fattened with other people's approval. None of us ever gets enough. But the more we get, the more we want, like the fat man eating to support his corpulence. It may be time to break off from our insatiable craving for strokes and learn to live on less. The gospel affirms to us that we, under grace and forgiveness, have God's approval. If we have that, what is our need to have such repeated human verification of the divine gift? Perhaps it is our refusal to claim our inheritance in the gospel.

Failure of Truth

Many of us fail to enter the freedom that is open to us as our inheritance because we choose not to give up some lie we are living.

Perhaps children have to learn to deceive in order to cope; at least they see it that way. I know a little girl of three who felt a need to conceal from her mother just how much she loves her father. There tends to be an assumption that the

mother would stop loving and caring for the child if that secret were fully discovered. So she asked, "Mommy, do you
know what I'm thinking when I'm thinking?" To this the
mother's answer was, "No, dear, I don't know what you are
thinking when you are thinking." The child's response was a
relieved "That's good!" This little girl had an inborn need to
conceal her thoughts from her mother, and she needed the
reassurance that mothers aren't mind readers.

Perhaps every child gets into the act of concealing his or
her private thoughts from their parents or any other authority that might punish or reject them because of what they
were thinking. On one occasion I was away from home for a
week. My late wife told me one of the children had been
sick, and she let the child sleep with her. She and the boy
met me at the airport, and he gave unusual expressions of affection for me. In a half-teasing tone I said, "If you love me
all that much, why did you take my place in bed while I was
gone?" As quick as a flash he responded, "I love you in the
daytime and Mother at night."

In our childhood, we feel a necessity to bury our threatening ideas and fantasies like a squirrel burying nuts. My
child-of-the-past put them (purposefully) in a place where I
would never find them (unlike the squirrel). In fact, when I
put these thoughts and feelings into the dungeon of the unconscious, I told them that they must go into hiding so I
would never have to face them as long as I live. This puts
the child in me in a position to deny that such thoughts and
feelings ever existed. It also puts one in a position to deny
some big pieces of existence, not so much a verbal denial as
a way of life.

The need to conceal or deny gets reinforced at school and
on the playground. Some children have a field day with anything different or unusual. You can imagine what Adolf Hitler would have gone through if his playmates had worked
with his father's name, Schicklgruber—a name the father
changed before his son's birth.

So the child often learns from other children that it is safer to deceive, conceal, pretend, or do anything to avoid the sharklike attacks on one's peculiarities, secret warts or moles, or hidden birthmarks.

Many of us feel that we will be rejected if we are fully known, if all the truth is out. Hence we protect the submerged continent of our childhood with vigor, the vigor either of denial or of concealment.

Freedom to Be

Our birthright in the gospel is the freedom not to have to conceal what we once covered. It's a wonderful release of energy not to have to lie anymore, to know we can be accepted in spite of all that seems unacceptable about us. It comes with the awareness that we are like all the other human beings out there; they also have some demons in their history. In addition, we realize that these other people are very little concerned with our demons; rather, they are involved with their own. They are consoled, in fact, if they learn that we have a few.

Our desire to make ourselves seem to others to be a little different and a little better than we are is a continuation of our lie. The acceptance that we are who we are, including all our past and present, could be the start of zestful living, since we no longer have to lie about ourselves. We don't have to be threatened if our nickname gets out or if all our story becomes known.

The New Testament assurance that the Christ has authority over demonic forces means that his forgiveness and grace are very powerful. In fact, there is an energy exchange in being fully forgiven and fully accepted. That must have been the transaction in the lives of the early Christians; their liberation left them enough energy to reshape the world around them.

Chapter 7

The New Orbit of the Spirit

Our gift as a Christian is meant to free up energies once used to conceal who we are, to deny who we are, or to pretend to be what we are not: to deny the self in the wrong way. To deny the self that we are is not proper self-denial. Genuine self-denial may be denying ourselves the luxury of pretending to be what we are not.

The Unpredictable Orbit

Energy Conservation

First, we save a large amount of energy in no longer needing to carry a heavy shield of pretense. We get a second energy source in dropping the pretense, because this makes relating to others much easier. The third and largest energy gain is from accepting God's OK (and that of others). It is a surprising generation of new energies. This comes about because we are freed to move close to other human beings and are able to allow others into our space. The deeper we encounter another human being, the more we release energy in response to him or her. This principle is quite obvious between two lovers at the physical and emotional level. In other words, Romeo and Juliet hardly entered into a relationship of meaningful intimacy in one evening's courtship, yet each of them was dynamically affected by the chemistry in the close exchange.

I don't pretend to understand what happens, but I do know that when a small group gets intimate and close, every member receives new energy, new drive, more excitement, and more freedom and creativity. The renewed zest for living seems to come in proportion to the intimacy a group reaches. I'm not talking about physical intimacy or sexual intimacy but about the closeness that comes from lowering defenses and shedding pretenses. The very fact that we can really be accepted and loved without pretense is almost like a big inheritance. Not only do we save energy today, we know we will continue to save as much every day. What people do for each other was spoken by a member of a small group with whom I shared. He said that the loving, trusting attitude of each person in the group left him with the feeling of acceptance, along with the feeling that "what was being done in the group was also being done in heaven." In other words, the loving intimacy of the group gave him a feeling that he was moving closer to the nature of reality and truth. "The closer we all touched each other, the more we felt release." Perhaps the intent of the gospel is to increase this ability to get closer to one another as our walls of partition give way in the presence of the love and warmth of those who are truly accepting.

Perhaps my touching closer to human realities is roughly parallel to a law of physics that more energy is released with deeper probings of the atom. Perhaps Jesus did strike at the inner core of our nature with the purpose of releasing us to more creative involvement with each other. It was a human birthright among primitive peoples to have a group of relatives to whom one was bonded by both kinship and loyalty ties. It was necessary to life as they lived it to be welded together in mutual care and protection.

In saying "Call no man your father" (Matt. 12:9), Jesus seemed to be stripping away the ancient bonding that held social groups together. I doubt if he would take away such bonding unless he could offer a better one. Perhaps this is some of the meaning of Pentecost, where we have evidence of a new bonding power bringing peoples together from many ethnic backgrounds and languages—the power of the Spirit.

This new force let loose in the world is one of extreme potency. It does not bind people together in a mutual commitment to support the clan against the stranger and the foreigner. It is a spirit that is grieved when anyone is excluded. Again, it is an energy-releasing spirit, as you learn that others who appeared to be enemies are actually sisters and brothers. You no longer need to defend against them or fear their attacks when they are led by the same spirit.

A New Kind of Power

Our birthright as Christians does not give us *control* of a new source of energy and creativity so much as it gives flashes and sparkles in the encounter. We may be more like Benjamin Franklin, flying his kite in an electrical storm to touch a strange and still unharnessed energy.

Paul, in his prison days, yearned to stay close to "the power of his resurrection" (Phil. 3:10). If you believe in miracles such as healings and turning of water into wine, these are but a tiny particle of faith compared to a belief in resurrection!

Resurrection as miracle is radically different. This is something that doesn't *happen* in nature. It is beyond the scope of science to repeat it or even understand it. Resurrection is not the same thing as the cases of revival after short-lived death reported in hospitals and dentists' offices. If we are to take the reporting of the New Testament seriously, we are talking about an actual return from death many hours after the event. The persons reporting the event had first to be convinced of its reality.

It is doubtful if Jesus himself was in direct control of the resurrection power. He died *believing* it would happen, but apparently not *knowing* it would happen. So I do not see the apostle Paul trying to get hold, or control, of that power so much as he was trying to live his life toward the center or toward the reality whence that power flows. To touch it now and then might be enough to energize a human being.

The resurrection power, as measured by human devices, is not power at all. It is a potent, invisible reality that cannot be owned or possessed. If it were possible to control this power, we all would want some. Others would merchandise it to great profit. The men who set out to build the Tower of Babel must have considered that their success would put them in charge of this hidden power—it could mean no more vale of tears or valley of the shadow. They would finance the whole deal by selling advance spaces near the top of their tower. The elderly could then retire adjacent to heaven's portals, contributing all their earthly possessions as payment for some divine-human surgery that would appropriately separate soul and body at the last gasp.

The people of Babel were not the last ones to want to rid humanity of the fear of dying. This has been going on ever since in one way or another, and my desire to buy longevity at the cost of meaning can be my temptation to seize or buy some of the resurrection power. My desire to hold on at any cost is too costly.

If I am going to have a life of worth, I must be in process of turning the power loose. The more I clutch it, the more it gets away like a dream that escapes. But this all sounds very paradoxical, turning loose of control, letting go, breaking free, floating without a rudder, dropping my defenses. Aren't we taught to get in control, to be careful about trusting, to hold on to what we've got, and to beware of con artists?

Really, it is proper to be as wise as the serpent, but necessary to be as harmless as a dove (Matt. 10:16). The power you give up as a Christian is the offensive weaponry of attack such as that of the serpent with venom. The dove as a symbol of peace is also a symbol of the Spirit. The power of doves is their sensitivity to the hidden power behind the scene—the power from which flows the little clusters of power called nations or dynasties. Paul says all such power (or authority) is from God (Rom. 13:1), even when these powers do not themselves know it. With the wisdom of the serpent, you know where the power center is, even when human power denies the source. Also, a part of the serpent's wisdom comes in not letting it be known what you know. The ability to conceal your wisdom is often the better part of wisdom. It takes little energy to conceal the truth, while it takes much to conceal falsehood.

The ultimate center of power then is outside the range of human control or ability to manipulate. Yet it is not beyond our ability to touch and be touched by it. None of us has a guaranteed channel of communication with God, one that works directly, like a two-way radio. None of us has control of the action of the world of the spirit. We cannot direct the power of the flow; we can only be submissive to a power that may or may not flow through the channel we reserve for it. Sometimes it does, usually it doesn't. Maybe this is to let us know that we are not in charge of the hidden power, and that we cannot even know the laws that govern its flow pattern.

I'm speculating that the spirit world is so mysterious to us that its existence is like a comet that cuts across the orbits of planets and stars and yet comes blazing into our view often enough that we have to deal with it. It troubles us because it does not have an orbit we can predict or a behavior we can control, yet it is there—occasionally.

The Hidden Power Source

The Silent Power

It is a faith assumption that this occasional appearance of the light and the power is a sign of more to come and that it is the power behind the universe, the one that ultimately shapes the course of events. I say ultimately, yet it does not seem to be at work at all when judged immediately. The words of Shakespeare are appropriate when he has Hamlet say, "There's a divinity that shapes our ends, rough-hew them how we will." The "end" here represents the ultimate. The ultimate power is seldom the obvious power.

The world of the Spirit does not seem to impose itself. It seems to restrain itself from interrupting when earthly powers go awry, make bad choices, or pursue evil courses. The Spirit remains silent when earthly powers seem to be ultimate, such as dictators like Nero and Hitler. It allows them to play their game out to the end. The end always reveals that their game was one of pretense. The Spirit seems not to rush the day of revelation, of uncovering the conceit of those who pretend to be in control of history, or of those who believe their own pretense, such as Herod, Stalin, or Idi Amin.

The faithful are often left wondering why the Spirit does not intervene, interrupt, or even destroy the forces of evil when they run rampant over the innocent. That question waits for a better answer than you or I can give now. We may never be able to answer it in this phase of existence, because we still are not in touch with the center of spiritual reality. Even "Christ after the flesh" died posing the question "Why?" We might speed up the process if we were able to enter into the sufferings of the victims of brutality and senseless shootings that occur almost daily around us.

All this brandishing of the powers of evil could lead one to think that truth and right are twin brothers of misfortune. The ancient question of the psalmist repeats: "Why do the wicked prosper?" Or the question of Job: "Why do the righteous suffer?" The winnings of the wicked could make us repent our virtues rather than our sins. It could dull our hope and trust in the hidden power of truth.

Truth: Concealed and Revealed

Jesus called the Spirit "the Spirit of truth." He said that the work of the Spirit was to reveal many hidden things. This implies that the ways of the Spirit are a reversal of the natural process in human relationships. In other words, human beings conceal the evil, while the Spirit conceals the truth and wants to share it as we are able to receive it.

It was the ancient assumption that whoever brought the truth of the gods to men would be punished by the gods. Prometheus brought the fire of the gods (truth) to earth, so he was chained to a rock in the Caucasus, where an eagle picked out his liver by day as it grew back each night. The story of Jesus is a reversal of the Greek myth; the punishment for bringing the truth of God to earth was at the hands of humans. "Light is come into the world, and men loved darkness rather than light" (John 3:19, KJV).

The love of darkness is revealed repeatedly in history as the searchers for truth have been resisted: Galileo, Charles Darwin, Sigmund Freud. I wonder what the next big breakthrough will be. I also fear that I will lead the fight against having any more light shed upon all that it means to be human, limited, and mortal.

It is almost a given fact that if we are to discover some of the hidden pellets of truth, we will have to suffer in the process. The more the truth is about human beings, the more resistance. The same if the truth is about God. Jesus revealed much about both God and humans. One truth is that people resist the light of truth because they *assume* the light to be judgmental and critical. Jesus said the light was loving and forgiving. That was resisted, not because it was not good news but because it was too radically different from what had always been believed. Actually, it was too good to entertain!

Then what about a power or a system of organization that has no seniority? "Many that are first will be last, and the last first." What about the kind of lord of the manor who pays

the same wages to those who work one hour as to those who
work all day? I wonder if we could tolerate a non-merit-
badge order?

Does something inside you twist in discomfort when the
last are put first? A lad from a black sharecropper family
turned out to be a mathematical genius and went to Colum-
bia University in recognition of that genius. He became a
university president, surpassing all the people of his village,
white or black, in power and influence. This story, in one
way or another, is always being dramatized. When it happens in your village it upsets the status quo to a painful degree.

If you lived next door to a man who showed the partiality
to his second son that the father of the prodigal son showed,
how do you think you would react when the party was given
(Luke 15:11-32)? Suppose you had moved to the farm next
door a year after the prodigal's departure and for a period of
ten years had never seen the father smile once. Also, you had
never been inside his home in all this time. Now, all of a sud-
den, you get a hurry-up invitation to come over one evening
for a big feast and dance. In the meantime, you have gotten
well acquainted with the elder brother and know he is constantly trying to return the smile to his father's countenance,
all to no avail. You make suggestions to him as he shares with
you his concern for his father's health and his fears that the
grief and depression over the prodigal son will kill him. By
the time the prodigal returns, you are already angry at him
for the way he has treated his family. And now to be asked
to celebrate his return as if this father had only one son!
Maybe this touches on what the Greeks called the "divine
madness."

I suppose we are all threatened when God's face shows, re-
vealing a new order of reality that does not fit in with the
flow of things as they normally are. It represents a reversal
of much of the flow of time and experience. It selects the
younger over the elder, it puts the last first and first last.

Suffering

There are several reasons why we must suffer in order to know truth. First, we suffer in having to change our assumptions. For example, if I have thousands, even millions, of pieces of data in my mind stacked around the assumption that the earth is flat, there's no way I am going to change that assumption without great resistance. It costs too much energy to reorder so many pieces of experience and update all of them. It would be like going through a library and rewriting all the physics books that are pre-Einstein.

Another reason we suffer to get at the truth is its hiddenness, in almost every sphere from mathematics to philosophy. It took struggle along with commitment and dedication for Thomas Edison to master the principle that made the electric light bulb possible. Then we risk the rejection of our friends if we embrace a truth before it is widely accepted. In fact the truths of sociology and psychology are usually tested in arenas of human resistance. To be in touch with the hidden powers begins with a belief that the world of spirit, though chiefly concealed, still holds the key to ultimate truth and reality.

In applying this idea to the life of the apostle Paul, we see his encounter with truth as the thing that drove a wedge between "Saul" and "Paul." His life had been that of the zealous rabbi, loyal to his traditions and compelled to uphold them against every threat. At the peak of his zeal, he had his own orbit crossed by the light of the gospel. This light blinded him with its brilliance, for it was the cornerstone for rebuilding his life. When you have just finished building your big house, it is a great suffering to have it torn down and have to begin again. It is an even greater suffering to lose all your friends and supporters and have them turn into enemies. Then begins the slow process of making friends with all those who considered you an enemy. It is certainly a more total about-face than changing from Republican to Democrat or from Baptist to Catholic.

Our Portion in the Spirit

What Reward for Us?

Perhaps we are fortunate that we didn't have the clash with truth and reality that the apostle Paul had, one that spun life over into a new orbit all in one encounter. For most of us the encounter is more gradual, giving time for us to phase down before turning in a completely different direction.

We perhaps speculate on what we will get as our reward if we give up certain things in order to follow faithfully toward the truth as we see it. The apostle Peter asked Jesus, in effect, "What do we get?" (Matt. 19:27). James and John wanted a guarantee about places of power and respect in the new order, "one at your right hand and one at your left" (Mark 10:37). The apostle Paul, reflecting on his achievements as a rabbi, was willing to count it all "refuse," garbage, in order that he might be in relation to Christ (Phil. 3:8ff.), the thing that symbolized his inheritance in the Spirit.

The reward for following Christ is what it has always been: the right to be in his company, to be near the truth, to enter closer to the hidden realities. This happens for those who pay the price, whatever is exacted of them, to be a part of the family of the faithful. And the people of faith are those who look in belief to the hidden power sources. They do not get trapped or deceived into thinking that what you see is what you get.

As a person of faith, I hope for what I can never see. I trust, in spite of all the misfortune, illness, or evil around, that God has not given up—indeed, does not give up—on us human beings and the messes we make. Faith is fruitless if I attempt to substitute a future that I project for the one that God plans. Faith also fails if I try to trade my earnings and assets for spiritual advantage. The material world and things material can keep us earthbound; the faithful usually travel light. We can't make material values absolute without forfeiting our wings, and maybe our song.

We measure the value of material things by the principle of scarcity. We measure things of the spiritual dimension by the principle of abundance—for example, the beauty of the endless sea, the numberless stars of the sky, or a billion bluebonnets. It takes the abundance of nature to get us started in the spiritual direction of a grace that is superabundant.

It seems to be the intention of the Spirit to give us all things.

Material Substance

It might seem to you that I have made light of earthly ownership of things of substance. I have not intended to do so. The Spirit is not antimatter or antimaterial. The Spirit is set against our dealing with matter as having ultimate or final value. Of course matter has value. It is not to be scorned; in the beginning of the creation God blessed it all and called it good. What he called evil was the human inclination to make little gods out of created things, as if they could carry lasting worth and dignity. Material things cannot bear such significance, nor can they transcend themselves. The material order is limited to its own orbit and its own values. Gold does not set its own price; that is done by human markets governed by the principle of supply and demand. It all depends on how badly people want gold at a given time—human greed may stand behind it all.

It is not an evil thing that scarce goods bring a higher price. Evil enters when you and I mistake economic value for spiritual value and put the economic first. The fact that Jesus said "Man shall not live by bread alone" did not imply that we could live without bread. He accepted the fact that bread is necessary and included it in the model prayer. He dealt with bread by blessing it, giving thanks for it, and making it part of the communion of saints. He hallowed the commonplace things of life and lifted them up in thanksgiving and celebration. He touched the little experiences of daily existence and filled them with wonder and glory. But the lesson here is that the glory of earthly things needs the touch of the higher order. These things do not sparkle in their own right, but await whatever it was that made the bush burn for Moses or the star shine for the Wise Men.

Chapter 8

Your Heritage as Foundation

Except for the forgiving grace of God, I doubt if any of us could allow the past to simply be what it is. As human beings we carry all the scar tissue of our history. The big redwoods of California show the marks of fire and drought of hundreds of years. So our scars are reminders of the ills "that flesh is heir to." In addition, there are our marks and bruises of failure, of violence, of conflict, as well as the vapor trails of evil, selfishness, and thoughtlessness. We have no way of clearing the record written into our emotions, but for us, as Christians, the power of the past can be defused in grace and forgiveness.

Our Spiritual Heritage

Trust of the Past

As a young man, I got the notion that to be a really good Christian I would need to get rid of my own history and start life completely afresh. Kierkegaard once thought he would, in becoming a Christian, get a "brand-new self," but he went on to say that what he got was "the old one I wouldn't have picked up from the road." This is a way of saying that the intent of the Spirit is to give continuity and flow to life rather than set up discontinuity and division in the stream. However, we all need to break with the past, leave it, venture forth, risk losing it, in order to find the meaning of it. It feels like drag and curse and embarrassment until we leave it far enough and long enough to be able to come back to it—with grace. Grace helps us take all our history back upon ourselves. Spiritually we cannot develop the basic trust about who we are until we claim all the past as essentially ours, both what we like and what we dislike. But the threat to our pride could make us want to conceal the scars of embarrassment or failure: "It is now in the interest of pride that the past should be something entirely left behind" (Kierkegaard, p. 183). As long as we feel compelled to rise above our past or to deny its reality, we consume unnecessary energies and are on guard against being fully revealed. Having it out or having little investment in keeping our past concealed means that we trust our sisters and brothers enough to allow them to know us. This may in turn allow them to let down some of their defenses in greater self-acceptance. In it all, we hope, there is an increase in relationship.

Trust of the Future

Without the basic trust of life, we have difficulty turning water into wine. We not only need to trust ourselves and others regarding our past but also regarding our *future*.

There is no way for me to word the threat under which we live in the present scientific/military potential for destruction and desolation of the only living space we have. The very fact that we can go on living in the face of such ominous and bodeful realities is itself an occasion for hope, a sign of a deep trust in the ultimate ability of God to deliver his promises to us. There is no guarantee that a perversion of scientific genius by power politics will not destroy us all. A greater question is one of how we will use our trust in God's goodness as a way to help us out of this man-made wilderness of terror and fear. Certainly you and I need to get beyond the scapegoating that puts blame for our mess on those who are different. Our basis for trust is not in ourselves but in God and his ability to deliver us from ourselves (we are part of the enemy). With God's help and guidance, we can live in the trust that when we gain power over others, we will use it not only for our advantage but also as a way of relating creatively and meaningfully. We cannot make life better for ourselves unless we are committed to making it better for our neighbor. The same is true of happiness; the more we bring happiness to others, the more we have it ourselves. The more we take happiness away from someone else, the less we have. This same rule may reverse when it comes to material values. Material value increases with scarcity; spiritual values increase with plenty. "Give, and it will be given to you" (Luke 6:38) was spoken of gifts of the Spirit such as joy, mercy, peace, and happiness. It is in pouring out our last drop of these treasures that our cup fills up again. It takes trust and commitment to empty ourselves for the needs and hungers of others. It occurs to me that the feeding of the five thousand was uniquely set up by a child who braved his hunger, trusting his lunch to whatever Jesus would do with it. I don't know many children who would share their dessert, much less their whole meal! Yet sharing what we have opens the door to sharing the self and may open the door to miracle.

Trust in God

God can be trusted; he is about the work of helping us grow toward maturity. His plan often carries us through much testing and adversity, even disappointment, grief, and failure. All the negatives can be building blocks in the house of human character. God is not known to be wasteful with resources. Jesus insists we can trust God to "give good things to those who ask him." Jesus says if your son asks for a loaf, you do not give him a stone that looks like a loaf. If he asks for a fish, you do not give him a serpent that looks like a fish. Jesus makes the case that if we humans would not betray our children with deceitful giving, how much less would God do so. Just as we are concerned to give our children things that make for character and endurance, so God offers us, not all the things that delight us but some things that stretch us. Some of us get stretched more than others. Some of us enter stretching experiences as volunteers; others are called on, with no choice. The only choice we often have is whether we will learn from painful processes or whether we will despairingly endure them. It is not so much the experience itself that spells either tragedy or stepping-stone in our lives as it is the way in which we *react* to the experience. If we seek to learn and grow, we increase our trust in God to be faithful, "now and at the hour of our death."

Developing Christian Character

From Flabbiness to Firmness

Faithfulness to God and the self is a desire and a commitment to grow toward greater maturity. It is to outfit ourselves for the spiritual journey as if we would prepare for a space voyage where special equipment is required. We are "getting ready to meet the saints." In preparing for the future, it is important that we make our place among the "saints" here and now. The way we prepare is in a living with, relating to, being frustrated by the saints in our community. None of them has yet reached a stage of perfection. In the words of C. S. Lewis, our aim is to become "solider and solider."

The apostle Simon Peter may serve as an example of what grace expects to do with us. As we recalled earlier, Jesus renamed Simon, son of John, as Peter, meaning "rock." Jesus knew that the trials and pains of the apostolic walk would turn this compulsive talker into a steadfast, dependable leader of the early Christian community. Greedy Zacchaeus became the generous giver; harlots became women of purity; and the cowardly became brave, rejoicing that they were thought worthy to suffer for the faith.

Granted that the encounter of a person with the grace of God often shows a radical change in that person, sometimes turning her or him into the opposite of what was seen before. However, just because there is a dramatic change in a person does not mean the person is separated from the past and given only a spiritual history.

From Persecutor to Persecuted

The apostle Paul is an example of one whose history, when it got refocused, made him the dynamic evangelist, teacher, prophet, and writer. Without his theological background as a highly schooled rabbi in the rich traditions of his Jewish heritage, Paul would probably have been only an ordinary convert. As it was, he built again the things he had torn down. This meant that in demolishing the little pockets of people devoted to the worship and service of Christ, he discovered what tough timbers the early churches were made of. Even his labor of tearing down churches was, oddly enough, his preparation for rebuilding them! In the economy of God, the new Paul incorporated and used all that had been "Saul" in the past. The break between the past and the present was healed, and the whole person that was Paul became involved in a total way in the Christian enterprise. There is no indication that Paul did anything other than reveal all his past. He was regretful about his former life as a zealous persecuter, but all the painful facts were laid out. Paul's own radical change of direction became a testimony that God, working through grace, seeks to turn defectors into witnesses, prisoners into watchmen, doubters into believers, and the worldly into worshipers. As in the case of Simon Peter, the Spirit works with resources at hand to turn people into their opposites—the coldhearted become enthusiastic, the weak become strong, the fearful courageous, the stutterers become spokesmen, and the empty become filled.

In my own experience in battle, the fellow soldier who most feared beforehand that he would be a coward came off with a silver star for bravery. Christian character is revealed under such pressure when persons have to make a choice between their own lives and the lives of their companions. Many of us saw the picture on TV in which a man threw himself into the icy waters of the Potomac River to save the life of a woman victim of the Air Florida airliner crash. If he had had a long time to think about doing something, the story might have been different. He acted spontaneously in the interest of saving someone's life, not thinking of his own life first.

From Material Value to Spiritual Value

Christian character essentially moves us in the direction of putting ultimate value on other human beings without asking questions about their age, sex, race, or station in life. As human beings, any human beings, they hold infinite value for God. We begin to take on some of the character of God when we place such value on other persons. Oddly enough, when we value others highly, we also add to our own worth in our own eyes.

I mentioned the soldier who won the silver star for bravery. This came about when he braved the night, the rain, and the heavily mined woods to get a patrol together and pick up those of his comrades wounded from mine blasts. When asked how he could muster the courage to walk into what seemed certain death, he answered, "Of course I thought I would get killed, but it was better to die than live with myself listening to those guys crying out in the night the rest of my life." To be sure, his act was one of great bravery, but that bravery was the expression of a conscience that had been shaped by spiritual nurture and Christian values.

In my city there was a notable example of Christian character displayed. A woman of fifty-four discovered that her son had been involved in a robbery that led to a murder. She heard on the news the description of her car and knew her son had been driving the car at the time. As soon as she confirmed the facts, she took her son to the police station and turned him in. When asked if she had had a great struggle deciding whether to do such a thing, she replied, "My mama always taught me to do right." She indicated that there was no option open to her; she felt compelled to do the right thing. Of course that woman did the best thing possible for her son, but the last thing he wanted her to do. Certainly she did the hardest thing any mother could ever do.

From the Heroic to the Daily Tasks

In these cases, you have looked at acts of bravery and courage in life-and-death situations. What about the show of Christian character on the daily scene? What do you exact of yourself? What if the IRS made a mistake and doubled your refund check? Would you go through the red tape to give the money back? What about the extra dollar the new cashier gives you at the grocery checkout? Can you give it back without embarrassing her and jeopardizing her job?

Take another situation: Do you tell the truth about the ages of your children, especially if they get in for half fare if you fib a little? What about your company's tools, cars, machines, or paper clips?

Perhaps the discipline of good Christian character begins with the way we manage or mismanage the truth. Can people be sure that what we say is the way it is? Do we tell the truth about the cost of things we buy—houses, cars, clothes? Do we do what we promise to do, beginning with being there? Are we careful to be on time with repayment of debts? If a friend lends me five dollars, do I remember to repay as I had promised? Do I make more promises than I have time or resources to fulfill? If I am in debt with my promises, what am I doing to the trust of other people?

Flaws in character structure begin with not telling the truth plainly and simply. A second flaw is revealed if we cover failure with untruth. I suppose that we all pretend (or lie) a little here and there. But if we reach the point that we put up a second pretense to cover the first, it may be time to deal with these flaws. No permanent spiritual house can be laid on that sort of foundation. If we build on it, we are the first to know and we will dread most the flood or wind of life that one day reveals our foundation to be sand instead of rock.

From Pretense to Honesty

In addition, if we are careful to build Christian character in our children, it is important not to bring them into any game of pretense, a pretense that things are OK when they are not, that they are super when in fact they are falling apart. The next step is not allowing our children to draw us into their pretense with their peers should they get into some big game of make-believe. I'm not saying that *all* pretense is bad. Sometimes a bit of it is necessary in order for us to cope. But our children know if a pretense is very important to us and they will resent continually having to keep our pretenses going. They will usually make us pay for their being used in any such way. I knew a situation where a sixteen-year-old girl got what she wanted from her father because she learned his secret accidentally. She never openly threatened blackmail; she didn't have to!

It is never too late to be honest, to go back to the point where you departed from the truth and deal with all the deceit that followed. One man, when faced with his years of double-dealing, was not willing to change. He told me his truth would expose too many others, several of whom might do him bodily harm if he tried to go straight. Like Macbeth, who, having murdered so much, found it easier to continue his course than to opt for a new beginning, he thought it was too late to change.

The miracle is still possible—the miracle of grace in which the dishonest suddenly become honest and thieves become good stewards. Usually, however, Christian character is much slower in forming. It occurs by discipline and slow growth, by hard effort and sacrifice, by pain, struggle, and self-denial. Nature gives us our first face; character shapes us after age forty.

Sharing the Inner Space

My Need for Others

A part of developing Christian character is realizing that we grow best in a community of others, not in isolation. Attempting to reach maturity alone is a feeble move; genuine growth depends on our sharing our lives with others. Here is an example of how *not* to manage your interior space.

Mark S came to me for counseling eighteen months after he lost his wife of twenty-three years. He said he suffered intolerable spells of loneliness and had no one with whom he could share. He was left with two teenage children: a daughter, sixteen, and a son, fourteen. He had moved into his parents' house; his job required help with the children, so this was very convenient. In addition, his parents had encouraged him to return home. Mark himself was an only child.

Since he spoke first of his loneliness, I asked if he had been able to share his life in an intimate sense with his wife while she was alive. He responded that he felt they had always been rather close, but really she never got into the deeper area of his feelings. In fact, he felt a great deal of guilt that he had never been able to let his wife know him as he actually was. It was as if he held a "holy of holies" within his interior life. I asked him if anyone had ever gotten into his most private space. His answer was, "The closest anyone ever got into that area was my mother, and perhaps my daughter, just a little." Neither mother nor daughter had reached the middle of his private space; they had only touched a corner of it. In his own fantasy, he said, he was keeping that most private space for God to enter; it seemed only fitting to him that he should have a space reserved for God only.

Jesus Wants Company

Before Jesus would enter our private space, I feel convinced he would say, "Go, call your husband" (John 4:16) or "Go, call your wife." Even God does not seem to seek a private space with us. He seems unwilling to enter such a space, marked "for God alone." God actually wants to join us "where two or three are gathered" (Matt. 18:20), not where we are alone. God has given us the neighbor as our task. If we fail in that relationship, we may get a few more for practice. However, the hope that it is easy to relate to God may be a false hope, especially if we skip past the neighbor as one of our essential tasks. The fact is that if we have intimately related to our neighbor, we have learned to relate to Jesus. Jesus makes common cause with the neighbor and shares the same space. I also assume that he will enter no space that is shut to our neighbor.

This may sound like a reversal of all your religious training. It is greatly different from my own. For many years I kept one room in my spiritual house reserved for God, feeling that if any human being touched it, God would not occupy it. I was wrong. He seems to come where there is at least one other. Before we can dedicate or celebrate any private space, we are reminded that "God is no respecter of persons." He seldom favors us with special and private visitations. What he has to say to us is not a secret. He will give us truth that is for all the others. Anything God gives me by myself is not for me alone; it is for the "church," the group, the community of faith. This is the problem Paul had with those speaking in tongues. "He who speaks in a tongue edifies himself, but he who prophesies edifies the church" (I Cor. 14:4). It is not that the individual does not receive revelations from God, but that these are given not to single out someone for special privilege but to single out that person as bearer of truth to the church.

Having a private source of inspiration and truth that others do not share would be about as valuable as having an abundant supply of coins that are not legal tender. What God gives us seems always to be for sharing. This may not be the case with what we inherit from our families. What we inherit we often want to keep and treasure as our very own unique possessions. Perhaps the contrast between an earthly inheritance and the gifts of the Spirit would lead us to the conclusion that we can't have both. I will not put earthly holdings in complete opposition to spiritual gifts. However, if the earthly inheritance becomes the foundation for life and hope, then it does become an alien power to our spiritual growth.

The world is not itself God's enemy and a thing to be despised. It becomes a problem when we treat it as the be-all and end-all of existence, when we lift up the transient and passing scene as if it were forever. Perhaps we clutch it so that we have no room in hand or heart for spiritual gifts that go beyond our ability to imagine.

Jesus gives us a paradox about his relationship to us. On the one hand he says, "I go prepare a place for you" (John 14:2). But again, referring to the remainder of our earthly journey in the same chapter, he speaks of coming together with the Father to "make our home with him" (John 14:23).

I once thought this meant that God and Jesus would come to dwell in the place I prepared for them. I no longer believe I can have that kind of private claim, even though I once hoped so.

If we apply the rule already expressed, we can have the divine presence on condition that we remain open to sharing our space with the human other. How could the rest of us handle our jealousy if one of us was singled out to have a private audience with God?

I am not discouraging personal and intimate sharing with God in private devotions. Certainly there are things we need to work out in our lives in God's presence. It is important, however, that our prayer agenda include the needs and concerns of all our sisters and brothers. It is also important that we come to place their needs alongside our own.

Our heritage, our personal and family history, our experience, failures, and griefs are all a part of us when we come into God's presence. The intention of the Spirit is one of binding all that we are, have been, and hope to be into a whole. Wholeness of person makes us ready to partake with our spiritual relatives in the New Creation.

Chapter 9

Your Inheritance
and the New Order

When the rich young ruler asked Jesus what he must do to inherit eternal life, I assume that Jesus told him to go get rid of his first and earthly inheritance. If you are a wealthy person, you are likely to ask if Jesus is saying the same to you. Yet you don't have to be wealthy to wonder. The poorest among us could put any heirloom ahead of brothers and sisters. That could be a chair, a table, a piano, or even a spoon. Whenever you or I prize a gift from the past above present relationships, we may need to go and sell our inheritance in order to get our values in line.

Earthly Ownership

Owning Instead of Being Owned

A part of Christian maturity comes in managing what you and I own in such a way that we do not become a slave to it. We have all seen people become owned by their material goods, even before they obtained them. This occurs when the "deceitfulness of riches" is consuming. I saw it happen to a man I knew when I visited him before surgery in a hospital. He was a professional man, but he worked at real estate on the side. In one short visit his phone rang three times, and he closed three business deals in summary fashion. If he could keep his mind on his profession, on his family, and on his friends with all that was happening, he's an exception! In my own case I confess that dabbling in the stock market interfered with my spiritual nurture. The stock page became too important; I had to buy an extra paper to give it double daily scrutiny, in addition to tuning in to the radio several times a day to check the Dow-Jones average. Most people who buy stocks, I admit, don't get that kind of fever. They can buy a stock and forget about it, but not me! I have to keep my hand on all the indicators, like a nurse checking a patient who has an irregular heart rhythm. God did not intend for us to get so absorbed in what we own, or hope to own, that we miss out on "the riches of his glorious inheritance in the saints" (Eph. 1:18). We need to wear earthly ownership loosely so that it doesn't require a wrecking bar to pry us apart from it in the end.

Another way of knowing whether we prize material values too much is whether we insist on being known by what we own. This can be anything from the clothing we wear to the auto we drive to the house we live in. It can include the clubs to which we belong or our ability to associate with those who are known either by their possessions or by their high lifestyle. Most of us will have friends up and down the scale of affluence. My question is whether we allow a person's financial status to determine our friendship. I have friends whom others consider rich. But I like to think that our friendships rest on our ability to be intimate and relational. I also like to think this would continue if we all became very poor in terms of earthly possessions.

Infinite Passion for the Finite

The "riches of his grace" are for us if we know that our earthly holdings are meager at most, that the greater treasures are free, that relationship is above ownership, that friendship is greater than bank accounts, and that friends can never be bought. All the great things that strengthen us in our pilgrimage through life are the things that are given. If you and I are fortunate to be among those who hold title to houses and land, stocks and jewels, all these things can be owned without getting in the way of intimate friendships and meaningful spiritual growth. Only we can determine if ownership costs us too heavily. Or do we worship just a little at some altar erected to things that are temporary? It may be for us as it was in the Gospel story of those making excuses regarding the great banquet—one had bought some new oxen; another, a parcel of ground; still another was on his honeymoon. So they all excused themselves from the ultimate and infinite occasion and gave passionate attention to temporary values. Is this not the meaning of a life fragmented? You and I become split apart unless we are drawn to that which is beyond us, that which is greater than we.

The self gets fused, integrated, made whole as we stretch toward the ultimate, which is always beyond our reach or grasp. The Spirit seems unwilling to bring us together as a whole around some earthly concern such as ownership, job, or social position. To be sure, all these things are good and they deserve energies, planning, and attention. We do not have to choose between them and spiritual values unless we allow them to give us a fever over their importance.

Examples of infinite passion given to finite things are found often in sports circles. When athletes were asked if they would take a certain injection if it would help them win an Olympic gold medal but cost them their lives in a couple of years, more than half of those questioned admitted they would take the injection. You have probably seen parents worship either their children or their children's activities; others show the same passion for politics, especially party politics. Some go after a hobby with the zeal of a saint praying for forgiveness. The commercials on radio and TV often show outstanding stars of stage or screen spending their most serious words on a diet drink or an insect powder. Don't misunderstand me, I want my roaches taken care of, but not with the same unction my minister uses to deal with the Sermon on the Mount on Sunday morning at eleven o'clock.

The Other Reality

The Place of the Material Order

Your material inheritance and your heritage are unique to you. What you receive from your past is different from the heritage of any other person alive or dead. That all adds up to your being, your identity as a person. It helps you answer the question, "Who am I?" Christian growth depends on having all of your self available. It also depends on your decision to be who you are with a commitment to become the one you are able to become. Becoming a self still implies building upon the self you already are, not departing from it, rejecting it, or avoiding it. Paul Tillich affirms (p. 20), "The New Being is not something that simply takes the place of the Old Being. But it is a renewal of the Old which has been corrupted, distorted, split and almost destroyed. Salvation does not destroy creation; but it transforms the Old Creation into a New one."

What the Spirit makes is a remaking of what already exists, making the old new, making all things new. So spiritual creation prepares you for the New Order, not as a new self but as the old self made anew. The self made anew includes the act of bringing everything that is you into one whole, leaving nothing out, excluding none of the scars and warps of your past. They must all be included if the work of the Spirit is to be a healing and creative act.

Along with the act of making you a whole self goes the special gift of no longer having to deceive, pretend, manipulate, prove, or dominate. The gift of the Spirit is one of making it OK for you to be yourself, to claim your specialness on the one hand and to accept your incredible sameness with all other selves on the other.

Your participation in the New Order begins now, not out

there at the end of life. That Order is yearning to make all
things new: to remake, to renew, and to resurrect. The image I see is of a sack full of seeds ready to be turned into a
crop, or a heaping pile of iron ore waiting to be turned into
machinery. But the miracle of making a person whole is
much greater than any wrought by nature or technology.
That miracle suits you for being responsive to the world of
Spirit in a world that goes by another set of laws. It may be
likened to a hidden power source that overrides the normal
circuitry. The new source does not destroy or negate the present structure of things but, rather, alerts us to things that are
ultimate, eternal, indestructible.

Witness to the New Order

   Look at it another way. Jesus says that we can only see the
kingdom of God by responding to the Spirit as the key to
ultimate reality. In talking with Nicodemus, Jesus said, "The
wind blows where it wills, and you hear the sound of it, but
you do not know whence it comes or whither it goes; so it is
with every one who is born of the Spirit" (John 3:8). This is
the story of those who respond to the hidden power source.
They live out their lives on the plane of history like everyone else, but they are witnesses to the New Order. Jesus the
Christ has revealed some of the mystery of things to come.
His revelation has turned prisoners of earth into watchers.
He has revealed that God is indeed the Father waiting to give
us an inheritance beyond our ability to dream or conceive.
From the impossible dream there bursts upon us the possibility that the miracle of grace is pressing upon the creation
from every quarter, yearning to infuse it with power and
glory.
   Perhaps we as human beings are on guard against too much
truth and reality. From the start of life we begin building our
defenses against the bombardment of stimulation and against
an overload of data to be absorbed or sorted. There is always more than any human can assimilate. We come to adult-

hood with a set of defenses that screen out most of the pulsations that pound on us. This means that the more subtle the vibration, the less likely we are to be aware of it. Spiritual messages are usually subtle and low key. This may be some of the meaning of Jesus' words: "He that hath ears to hear, let him hear" (Matt. 11:15, KJV). He implies that there is a great blindness and deafness to the more subtle things of the Spirit. Jesus even claims that his mission is that of awakening the eyes and ears of the blind and deaf. John Donne was quite aware of this when he said that even though he prayed three times daily, he felt he had probably "prayed twice in my lifetime." He confessed that only rarely did he break through to spiritual perception, to being in touch with the New Order.

There are those who touch the hidden power source now and then. The people who touched it at the center are the saints, who used the encounter to make the rest of us aware that, for the eye of faith, there are incredible realities waiting to be seen or grasped. In the Bible stories there are "theophanic events" (Martin Buber) that mark powerful insight into the world of Spirit. Abraham seemed to have been moved in a more gentle acceptance and claim that God had it in his purpose to bless Abraham and, through him, "all the families of the earth." It took more dramatic form in the burning bush for Moses and the blinding light for Paul. Yet these encounters had ways of breaking through human defenses to make the world of Spirit open to our awareness.

It is doubtful if any human being can stand in the presence of continual revelation. It might be that you will want to pray *not* to be invaded by the divine presence. Usually we pray for an insight or an experience of the spiritual when we don't mean to ask for too much; we might shut it off if it comes as a downpour. Not many of us would want the burden of trying to convince neighbors or friends that God had broken through and given us a unique message to be communicated to them. Wouldn't we be in about the same pre-

dicament as Moses when he was trying to back up his vision
with more authority? Moses knew that Pharaoh would laugh
at his claim, just as most people would laugh at us if we came
saying God had revealed a truth to us for them to hear. They
would immediately ask us to show some credentials for such
a claim. Some would credit us with being a phophet because
they would be convinced by our sincerity; others would dis-
credit us and subpoena us to appear for an insanity hearing
set for Tuesday.

God Incognito?

Seeing Beyond the Surface

Your inheritance in the New Order may call on you to
take the risk to follow faith when it goes against reason. It is
faith that puts us in touch with the unseen and eternal. Hebrews 11, the faith chapter of the Bible, indicates that those
of faith are more attuned to the unseen than to the obvious
stuff of creation. Faith assumes that what is seen comes from
a hidden and unseen source.

The New Order is always concealed. It is for the eye or
ear of faith, not for the newspaper, screen, or stage. Those
who touch upon it know that they are blessed. Like a child
wanting to share the beauties of creation who calls Mother
to look, see, and enjoy, so those of the Spirit have the child's
longing to share the wonders with all the brothers and sisters everywhere.

Again, let me emphasize that most people who are not attuned to the influx of spiritual experience are well defended
against such. Perhaps their defense comes in being open to
material data to such an extent that nothing else has a chance
to be seen or heard. In other words, the star that spoke to
the Wise Men would be only an irregular celestial comet, or
the light Paul saw would be explained as an inclination to epi-
lepsy, only an internal flash against the optic nerve.

The Domain of Evil

The New Order seems to press against the world of material reality with another and deeper reality, asking to be heard or seen amid the noises of street and factory. This may be the case of the first being last, and the last first. Indeed, the physical comes before the spiritual, but it is not first in the final analysis. I suppose it is a fact that God can wait; he is in no hurry. He has nothing to prove, no need to vaunt his strength or to advertise his power. In fact, there seems to be a reluctance for him to demonstrate any of his qualities; it is as if he would yield on every side to the demonic forces that have the drive to boast, to conquer, to control, and to rule. This seems to be the strategy of the Spirit: to allow the powers of evil to defeat themselves, to have their day, to show their hunger, and to reveal their impotence. The essence of evil is its absence of identity, its bootlegging of spiritual realities to claim some substance and credibility. Its area of dominion is the material, but its ambition is that of winning a foothold in the Spirit world.

The New Order calls on us to prepare for a reality that excels over any reality we have seen or heard; it calls on us not to deny our being but to claim it; not to submit to the powers of evil that promise immediate success or a reality that is staged or imaginary but to claim the self, to claim our integrity, our worth, our own identity. In this we join a reality that inherits the world as it is and shapes it for things as they will become—the kingdom of God. That kingdom is in process of making itself felt in the lives of the faithful; it is never *in* hand yet always *at* hand. It presses on all boundaries but is unknown except to the eye or ear of faith.

The Dominion of Christ

It is the audacious claim of the New Testament that Jesus laid his hand on the key to the hidden source of power, the power that created and sustains the universe. When, as a child, I read the story of Jesus' trial before Pilate, I wondered why he didn't declare his eternal kingship and do the Superman trick of destroying his enemies in a dazzling show of power.

The more I press my questions, the more I realize that Jesus never meant to take the world by storm but by the principle of the leaven in the dough. He had no need to tell Pilate anything; his truth was not to be wasted where no ears were prepared to hear. Christianity was never meant to convince at first by an argument or even by a miracle. Jesus won his disciples by loving them before he began penetrating their minds with truths—truths that were, at the start, outrageous to reason.

The disciples expected at first to become partakers of a kingdom, one where Jesus would reign in splendor, perhaps surpassing the glories of David and of Solomon. His reign would put them all on the center of the stage. It would certainly carry material benefits and spiritual advantage. The disciples expected Jesus to be the one who would combine the best of both worlds. Yet when this hope had to give way to hidden realities, it must have been their love for Jesus that kept them on course. They held to an uncanny trust that he was not about the business of deceiving them, though they couldn't know where it was all leading until the giving of the Holy Spirit at Pentecost.

Imagine, after Jesus' crucifixion, the wait before Pentecost! Imagine the chaos of it, the fear. How could the disciples ever face their wives and families, who had too long suffered hardship because the breadwinners had invested their time and energies in an enterprise that more and more seemed doomed to failure? Imagine the despair the disciples shared as they waited, only because he told them to wait. Yet he probably knew they needed forty days just to purge themselves of their grief—not only over losing Jesus but over losing all the dreams they had built around him, those about wealth, power, politics, and an earthly inheritance. "What do we get?" "What will be our share?"

The disciples not only loved Jesus but also, in their three-year walk with him, they had learned to love one another. In that consuming love, everything else they dreamed, hoped for, fantasized, or otherwise projected gave way. None of the dreams could match the fact that these men grew to have a devoted and passionate care for one another. They found themselves living under the "new commandment. . . . By this all men will know that you are my disciples, if you have love for one another" (John 13:34-35). To put it another way, the apostles probably entered with high expectations, got very little material reward or public acclaim, but found human closeness they couldn't have imagined. My supposition is that they were able to drop their pretenses in the presence of the one who was himself the Truth. They were then able to move into each other's spaces with positive releases of energy. It took Pentecost to help them get purpose and direction for their place in the New Order.

The New Order, then as now, is not only what is coming in terms of promise and anticipation; its presence is the love we are able to share. If we love, we are already entering the promises of God because "God is love."

When we know more about love, we know more about God. I wonder if we are not all going to be shocked to learn that God is the most loving and humble person in the universe. A picture I have is one of God being himself incognito among all the people in heaven. Our task then will be that of seeing if we can figure out which one is God after talking to everyone on the celestial scene.

All Are First-born

The writer to the Hebrews uses his imagination to picture the scene of the inheritance of the saints. He contrasts the gathering of the Israelites before Mount Sinai in Moses' day with the gathering of those entering finally and fully into the New Order. The Israelites under Moses' leadership gathered before Mount Sinai that "burned with fire." Moses said, "I tremble with fear" (Heb. 12:21), and they could not endure the agony of that exposure to the glory.

Now for the contrast: "But you have come to Mount Zion and to the city of the living God, the heavenly Jerusalem, and to . . . the assembly of the first-born" (Heb. 12:22-23).

The gathering of the first-born implies that the great company of the redeemed is a company of those inheriting the promises. Now, the first-born is a symbol. This does not mean that only first sons are the ones to inherit; it means that *all* are first-born. God has no second-born, no rank or order by which some are included and others excluded. All have a "double share," as was promised in the old covenant to the first son. This means that God stops counting with the "first." Each is in some sense the first; hence, each is set to inherit fully. This is some of the meaning of the parable of the eleventh-hour workers. No matter what your order in the kingdom, you are always treated with utmost dignity and respect. No one is less because of sex, religion, race, background, history, age, or place in the family.

It is time now to summarize the task of the Christian in the pilgrimage toward the full inheritance.

Neither a glorious heritage nor a fat inheritance gives you a right to boast, and the absence of these gives you no right to self-rejection or self-pity. As a Christian you are called to affirm the past. You may need to take an inward journey to explore the underground foundations of your house. You need your sisters and brothers to affirm that you are OK in your history, just as you need to affirm them. You need to build on all that you have been, no matter what. You can't build on another's foundation. God didn't mean for you to junk your own in favor of another. He wants you to affirm his creation, beginning with yourself. Affirming your self and choosing your self is an act of Spirit, the starting place of the New Order.

Questions for Thought and Discussion

Chapter 1

1. What does it mean personally and spiritually to venture out?
   a. What might it mean never to venture from our place?
   b. How is our identity affected in venturing out? What are the results of never venturing?
2. What might be a false start at becoming a mature self?
   a. What is a temptation on the way to becoming a self?
   b. In your own history, what are some of the limiting factors that make it difficult to accept yourself?

Chapter 2

Can you discuss and elaborate the paradox of human selfhood?

Chapter 3

After reading Chapter 3 can you elaborate on the experience of parental partiality either in your own home on in your community?

Chapter 4

1. Do you know people who have trouble with their name?
2. Do you have a nickname you would share?
3. Do you know where you got your name?

Chapter 5

Do you know anyone whose inheritance controlled that person too much?

Chapter 6

Are you aware of abuses of freedom? What about the freedom to cheat on income taxes?

Chapters 7 and 8

What is one of the "lies" that we human beings defend too much?

Chapter 9

What does it mean spiritually to be a "first-born"?

Selected Bibliography

Brown, Norman O. *Love's Body.* Vantage Press, 1966.

Buber, Martin. *Between Man and Man.* Tr. by Ronald Gregor Smith. Macmillan Co., 1948.

Campbell, Joseph. *The Hero with a Thousand Faces.* Princeton University Press, 1968.

Erickson, Erik H. *Young Man Luther.* W. W. Norton & Co., 1962.

Grayson, David. *Adventures in Friendship.* Doubleday, Page & Co., 1910.

Kierkegaard, Søren. *The Sickness Unto Death.* Tr. by Walter Lowrie. Princeton University Press, 1941.

Madden, Myron C. *The Power to Bless,* 2d ed. Broadman Press, 1977.

Novak, Michael. *Ascent of the Mountain, Flight of the Dove.* Harper & Row, 1971.

Solzhenitsyn, Alexander. *A World Split Apart.* Harper & Row, 1978.

Steinbeck, John. *East of Eden.* Penguin Books, 1981.

Teilhard de Chardin, Pierre. *Hymn of the Universe.* Harper & Row, 1961.

Tillich, Paul. *The New Being.* Charles Scribner's Sons, 1955.